THE WORLD'S FASTEST SPOOKIEST SMELLIEST STRONGEST Book

Written by Jan Payne
Illustrated by Mike Phillips
Edited by Sally Pilkington and Sue McMillan

The WORLD'S FASTEST SPOOKIEST SMELLIEST STRONGEST Book

Buster Books

The material in this book was first published in 2008
by Buster Books in a hardback edition titled 'The World's Best Book'.

This paperback edition is fully revised and updated
and was published in 2012 by Buster Books,
an imprint of Michael O'Mara Books Limited,
9 Lion Yard, Tremadoc Road, London SW4 7NQ

www.busterbooks.co.uk

A CIP catalogue record for this book is available from the British Library.

ISBN: 978-1-78055-114-2

2 4 6 8 10 9 7 5 3 1

Created and produced by The Complete Works
St Mary's Road, Royal Leamington Spa
Warwickshire CV31 1JP

Printed and bound in August 2012 by CPI Group (UK) Ltd, 108 Beddington Lane,
Croydon, CR0 4YY, United Kingdom.

Papers used by Buster Books are natural, recyclable products
made from wood grown in sustainable forests. The manufacturing processes
conform to the environmental regulations of the country of origin.

CONTENTS

Introduction – 10

HUMAN ACHIEVEMENT

LIVING MARVELS

OUR AMAZING PLANET AND BEYOND

INTRODUCTION

This book aims to amuse, entertain and amaze you with the most excellent, outstanding and, quite simply, best things on our planet and beyond.

To get started with a bang, here is the world's best joke ...

A couple of hunters are out in the woods, when one of them falls to the ground. His eyes are rolled back in their sockets and he doesn't seem to be breathing.

The other hunter whips out his mobile phone and calls the emergency services.

'My friend is dead! What can I do?' he gasps to the operator.

'Just take it easy. I can help. First, let's make sure he's dead,' says the operator, in a calm, soothing voice.

There is a silence, then a shot is heard.

The hunter's voice comes back on the line and says: 'OK. Now what?'

In 2002, after a whole year of hilarious ha-hard work, scientists from the 'Laugh Lab' at the University of Hertfordshire, England, concluded that this was the best joke ever. People around the globe were asked to rate a group of gags on a scale of one to five. Some were rejected because they were thought to be too rude, and some because they didn't work when translated into different languages. The winner was this joke, which was submitted by a psychiatrist who lived in Manchester, England.

Do you agree with the scientists that this is the funniest joke you have ever heard?

No?

Well, you may not necessarily agree with all of the 'bests' that are in this book, either. Some 'bests' are fact and will not change, such as the longest range of mountains or the first man in space. Others are 'bests' that may have been bettered by the time you read this book – people will run faster, planes will fly higher and new buildings will smash existing height records. Then there are 'bests' that are a matter of personal opinion, like the unluckiest queen or the world's funniest joke – not everyone agrees.

What everyone does agree on, however, is that *The World's Fastest, Spookiest, Smelliest, Strongest Book* is a selection of the best, biggest, bravest, worst, weirdest, wildest, funniest, flashiest, furthest, hottest, highest, hairiest, longest, lowest, loudest, deepest, darkest, deadliest, smallest, smelliest, strongest, most expensive, most venomous, most popular things, people and places that the world has to offer – right here, right now.

And whether it is the world's best book ... well, that's for you to decide.

HUMAN ACHIEVEMENT

THE MOST AMAZING PEOPLE

THE TALLEST LIVING MAN

Sultan Kösen was born in Turkey in 1982, and began to grow at an alarming rate when he was 10 years old. This was because of a tumour in the part of his brain that controls growth. In 2012, Kösen underwent a new treatment to stop him growing. Officials have confirmed his height at 2.51 metres.

As well as being the world's tallest man, Kösen is also the proud owner of the biggest hands and feet in the world. His feet are an amazing 36.5 centimetres long and he has yet to find a car that he can fit inside. Another giant among men is Leonid Stadnyk, born in 1970 in Ukraine, in eastern Europe. Stadnyk is said to be 2.57 metres tall, but he has refused to be measured by officials.

THE TALLEST MAN EVER

Sultan Kösen is tall, but he isn't as tall as the tallest man who has ever lived. Robert Pershing Wadlow was born on the 22nd of February 1918, in Alton, Illinois, USA. He didn't stop growing until the day he died in 1940. Wadlow, like Stadnyk, suffered from a condition that affected his pituitary gland – which produces growth hormones – and he grew to 2.72 metres.

THE TALLEST ANIMAL LOVER

Before Sultan Kösen was declared the world's tallest living man, a man called Bao Xishun, a herdsman from China, held the title. Bao may only measure 2.36 metres tall, but his extra-long arms, measuring 1.06 metres, came in very handy in 2006, when some dolphins needed rescuing. The dolphins had accidentally swallowed some plastic while in their pool at an aquarium in Fushun, north-east China. Surgical instruments had failed to remove the plastic from the marine mammals' stomachs – so Bao was called in. With his arm protected from the dolphins' teeth with towels, he reached right into the stomachs of the sick animals to remove the plastic.

THE SHORTEST MAN

Chandra Bahadur Dangi lives in Nepal. He is just 54.6 centimetres tall, and was confirmed as the world's shortest man in February 2012.

Chandra, who is believed to be around 72 years old, was recently measured six times over the course of a day by officials from the *Guinness Book of World Records*. He took the title from fellow Nepalese contender, Khagendra Thapa Magar, who measures 67 centimetres.

THE TALLEST WOMAN

Yao De-fen, from China, is thought to be the tallest woman in the world. She was born in 1972 and is 2.33 metres tall.

Yao grew so tall because, like the world's tallest man, she had a tumour on her pituitary gland that caused her to produce too much growth hormone. An operation to remove the tumour failed to completely get rid of it. Growing so big so fast has caused a lot of other health problems, and Yao finds it very difficult to move around without using crutches – she is cared for by her mum, who is just 1.37 metres tall.

THE OLDEST PEOPLE

When Jeanne Calment died in August 1997, she was an astonishing 122 years old, the oldest (proven) human being in history. As a girl growing up in Arles, France, she met the world-famous artist Vincent van Gogh, who was a customer in her father's shop. Calment described van Gogh, who died in 1890, as 'dirty, badly dressed and disagreeable'.

Christian Mortensen was born in Denmark on the 16th of August, 1882 and died in California on the 25th of April, 1998, aged 115 years, 252 days. He is officially confirmed to be the longest-lived man ever. Mortensen put his long life down to drinking plenty of water, smoking the occasional cigar, staying positive and doing lots of singing.

THE HAIRIEST PEOPLE

Some people have thick hair covering their entire bodies. Their condition is very rare, in fact only about 50 'wolf people', as they are known, have been documented since the Middle Ages.

In 1547, a ten-year-old boy was given to King Henry II of France as a gift. The boy's forehead, cheeks, nose and ears were covered with long, dark-blonde fur. Pedro Gonzalez came from Tenerife in the Canary Islands.

People at Henry's court wrongly believed Gonzalez was half human and half animal, so they called him the 'Wild Man'. But Gonzalez was very intelligent. He quickly learned French and Latin and soon became a trusted servant at court.

Hairiness is not just a thing of the past. Today, two men named Larry and Danny Gomez from Mexico are known as the 'Wolf Boys'. The brothers have a very rare condition called 'hypertrichosis', which causes hair to grow all over their faces and bodies. They are covered from head to toe in thick, curly, black hair. Born into a poor family, the brothers joined the circus when Larry was nine and Danny was six. They perform acrobatics on a trampoline, and Danny does somersaults off a moving motorbike. They love the circus life, have a lot of friends and are happy being who they are.

THE FASTEST HUMAN BEING

On the 16th of August 2008, Jamaican sprinter, Usain Bolt, broke his own world record at the Olympic Games in Beijing, China. In the 100 metres final, he ran the distance in just 9.69 seconds, winning a gold medal. The world's fastest man broke his own record again in 2009, running 100 metres in 9.58 seconds at the World Championships in Berlin, Germany.

In the original Olympics held in Ancient Greece in 776 BC, a short sprint of about 192 metres was the first, and only, competition.

THE FIRST STRONGEST WOMAN

The 'World's Strongest Woman' contest was first held in 2001. The winner was Jill Mills of the USA. When she won the contest she walked over 90 metres carrying 65 kilograms in each hand, and she came top in the 'Car Lift' competition.

Mills became interested in weight-lifting as a little girl, when she used to watch her dad lifting weights at home. She would wait for everyone to go to bed so that she could try herself. She practised constantly and kept herself fit running several kilometres a day. By the age of 19, Mills says she was able to do 84 push-ups and 128 sit-ups, each in a time of under 2 minutes.

THE STRONGEST MEN

The annual 'World's Strongest Man' contest is an international athletics event, testing the strength of each competitor in a range of challenges from log-lifting to lorry-pulling. The first contest was held in 1977, at Universal Studios in Los Angeles, USA. That first year, former US Olympic weightlifter Bruce Wilhelm was triumphant, and he retained his title the following year.

In the current competition, events include the 'Pillars of Hercules', in which the men must support the weight of a 160-kilogram stone pillar with each arm, for as long as they can; the 'Atlas Stones', in which five stones, each heavier than the last, must be hoisted on to pillars; and the 'Vehicle Pull', to see who can drag anything from a tram car to a plane the furthest!

Iceland has won a whopping eight times in the competition – four wins each for Jon Pall Sigmarsson and Magnus Ver Magnusson.

THE GREATEST MINDS

THE MOST NOBLE NOBEL PRIZE

Alfred Nobel was born in 1833 in Stockholm, Sweden. In his lifetime he achieved many things. He was the scientist who invented dynamite. He was a businessman and a campaigner for peace. He believed passionately in making the world a better place.

In his will, Nobel donated much of his fortune to setting up the Nobel Prize. The first prizes were awarded in 1901, to reward the highest achievements in science, literature and work towards peace. A Nobel Prize is one of the most prestigious awards anyone can win.

In 2007, the Nobel Peace Prize was divided between two winners – the Intergovernmental Panel on Climate Change (IPCC) and a politician from the USA called Al Gore – for their work on climate change. Together they shared the £760,000 prize money.

THE MOST AMAZING MEMORY

Ten packs of cards (520 cards altogether) were shuffled and put before Andi Bell. With just 20 minutes to memorise them, he was able to remember all of them in the correct order.

Bell, the World Memory Champion in 2002, has a method. Before a memory challenge, he walks round London, taking note of important landmarks, such as the Houses of Parliament, the London Eye or Westminster Bridge.

When Bell memorises the packs of cards, he imagines each card is something from his walk – an animal, a fruit or a vegetable. In his mind, he places the cards in threes at the different landmarks. Then, when it is time to remember the cards, Bell imagines walking around London again, seeing the cards as he passes by the landmarks he has memorised.

THE GREATEST INVENTIONS

No two people agree on the same top inventions, but this list shows inventions and discoveries that have had effects on our world far beyond anything the inventors could have imagined.

THE WHEEL

The wheel has been around for thousands of years, yet some societies, such as Native North Americans, never had them. Instead they had to carry heavy loads around on their backs, or haul things on a 'travois'. This was a frame made from two sticks with animal skins stretched between, which could be dragged along by dogs. So wheeled vehicles were not used in America until the end of the 15th century, when they were introduced by European explorers.

No one knows who actually invented the first wheel. Most scholars think that it was first used by people making clay pots in about 3500 BC.

The earliest known wheel to be used on a vehicle for transport is shown in a mosaic that dates back to about 3200 BC. It was found in Mesopotamia, which is now an area of modern Iraq. Some experts think the wheel may have been invented 5,000 years earlier in Asia.

WRITING

Have you ever wondered why some things are called 'historic' and others 'prehistoric'? The only difference is that history was written about and prehistory wasn't. Until the invention of writing there was no way of keeping records or communicating over long distances. Two of the earliest forms of writing found to date come from the Sumerian people of Mesopotamia and the Egyptians. Both date from around 3300 BC. The Sumerians used a script known as 'pictographic writing' and was made up of pictures carved into stone tablets to represent words, while the Egyptians used hieroglyphics.

The first writing was adapted over the centuries, and 500 years later the Babylonians, Persians and Assyrians used pointed sticks to press wedge-shaped marks into wet clay. This is known as 'cuneiform'.

Later, papyrus made from reeds, parchment made from animal skins, and paper made from mulberry bark, were used to write on. Some of the first inks were made from octopus or squid ink and were used with pens called 'quills' cut from feathers.

PRINTING

The first printing press was developed by Johannes Gutenberg in Germany in the 1450s. Gutenberg invented moveable type, making individual letters from metal that were arranged in a wooden frame to form a page. After the page had been inked and printed, the letters could be reused.

Before printing, books were copied out by hand. This took a long time and meant that they were enormously expensive. As a result, few people could read or write. After printing, books became much cheaper and information could spread more rapidly.

THE MECHANICAL CLOCK

A French monk named Gerbert, who became Pope Sylvester II in 999, is often credited with making the first mechanical clock. Over the next few centuries, further modifications made clocks more accurate. Did you know accurate clocks are vital in navigation? Sailing east and west was no problem, as sailors could work out where they were by the position of the Sun. When travelling north and south, however, sailors needed to know the exact time at a fixed location in order to work out where they were. The man who achieved this accuracy in a portable clock was John Harrison from Yorkshire, England. His clock, known as H4, was tested on a voyage from the UK to the West Indies, departing on the 18th of November 1761, and arriving on the 19th of January 1762. The clock was only 5.1 seconds slow.

THE WORLD'S FASTEST

PLANE

The speed record for a plane was set in 2004 by NASA's X-43A Hyper-X. This unmanned hypersonic aircraft was designed to test an experimental engine called a 'scramjet' and reached a speed of Mach 9.6, which corresponds to a speed of approximately 11,265 kilometres per hour, nearly 10 times the speed of sound. The fastest manned plane was a rocket-powered aircraft called the North American X-15A-2 (shown here), which reached a speed of 7,258 kilometres per hour in 1967.

CAR

On the 13th of October 1997, Thrust SSC, a British jet car, drove faster than the speed of sound. Two days later, the World Land Speed Record was made official when the Thrust SSC completed two runs at an average speed of 1,227.99 kilometres per hour.

PRODUCTION CAR

On the 26th of June 2010, the Bugatti Veyron Super Sport became the world's fastest production car (which means a mass-produced car that can be driven on the street), reaching a speed of 431.072 kilometres per hour. The 1,200 horsepower Bugatti broke the previous record of 412.28 kilometres per hour (set by the Shelby SuperCars' Ultimate Aero in 2007) on Volkswagen's Ehra-Lessien test track in Germany.

TRAIN

On the 3rd of April 2007 a French double-decker train, one of their *Trains à Grand Vitesse (TGV)*, smashed the world record for a train running on conventional rails. It reached a speed of 574.8 kilometres per hour. Sadly, if you want one, it will cost you £22 million.

The speed record for all trains was set by a Japanese Railway magnetic levitation train (Maglev) in 2003. It reached a speed of 581 kilometres per hour.

BOAT

Ken Warby designed and built a boat he named *Spirit of Australia* in his back yard in Sydney, Australia. On the 8th of October 1978, the boat reached 511 kilometres an hour and broke Warby's previous world record. Despite many attempts at the record, no one has taken it away from him.

LIFT

The Burj Khalifa building in Dubai, which contains hotels and residential apartments, is the tallest man-made structure ever (see page 42) and has the world's fastest passenger lifts. The building contains an impressive 57 lifts to take the tower's many visitors to the top. The quickest ones descend at a white-knuckle 64 kilometres per hour, or 18 metres per second. They are also the highest lifts in the world, and the highest shaft goes all the way to the top of the spearhead-shaped building.

THE WEIRDEST INVENTIONS

THE MOST UNLIKELY PORTABLE TOILET

Sometimes you need to get to a toilet fast, but now perhaps the toilet can come to you fast instead. Portable toilets are common, but what gives Paul Sender's invention an edge over its more stationary competitors is its 1,000-horsepower Boeing jet engine.

The toilet can reach a speed of over 110 kilometres per hour. You'd have to be pretty desperate to use it though.

THE ROLL-UP ZEBRA CROSSING

If you want to cross a busy road and there is no zebra crossing handy, stand on the kerb, unroll your own plastic black-and-white crossing and walk across. How you do that with lots of cars going by is not explained.

THE SAFEST COFFIN

Fear of being buried alive has pushed several inventors to come up with a 'safety coffin'. Some designs have included a vertical shaft leading from the coffin to an escape hatch at ground level.

Other coffins have had cords that could be pulled from inside the coffin, which were linked to alarm bells or waving flags above ground.

THE HAY FEVER RELIEF HAT

This handy hat includes a large toilet roll in a holder fixed on top of the hay-fever sufferer's head, so tissues are always to hand, but it's not a hat for those wish to avoid attention!

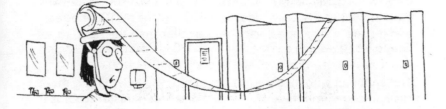

THE T-SHIRT BACK-SCRATCHING AID

This useful T-shirt has a map grid printed on the back of it. When the wearer has an itch, they can tell a friend exactly where it is. For example, they might request, 'Scratch my back at square C3, please'.

THE TEN-IN-ONE GARDEN TOOL

This tool, like a pen-knife, contains fold-out tools including a full-size fork, a spade, a hoe and a rake. Every tool the happy gardener might want is in this gadget. Unfortunately, it's much too big and awkward to lift, let alone use.

THE EMERGENCY TOILET SIGN

This sign can be carried in a backpack for emergencies. It has the word 'LADIES' and a stick-woman picture on the front of it and suckers on the back. When there's a queue at the ladies' toilet, you can stick it over the 'GENTS' sign next door and use that instead.

THE OLDEST THINGS
MADE BY MAN

THE OLDEST MONUMENT

One of the oldest monumental stone structures in the world is the Step Pyramid, built for King Djoser, a king of Egypt, who died in 2611 BC. Its base measures 120 metres by 108 metres, and it rises in six stages, each one smaller than the next, to a height of 60 metres.

The architect who invented the pyramid was an amazing man. His name was Imhotep, chief priest and first minister to Djoser. As well as being an architect he was also a skilled doctor (see page 33).

Pyramids were named after a cake! The monuments were called pyramids by the Greeks much later, from the name of a wheat-and-honey cake, called a 'pyramis' ('pyramides' is the word for more than one pyramis), which had the same square-bottomed shape.

THE OLDEST CLOCK

The earliest clocks date from around 1500 BC. Some used the Sun to divide up the day, as in a sundial, others used water. Water clocks measured the time taken for water to empty through a hole in a stone vessel. Mechanical clocks came much later.

The oldest working mechanical clock in the world that can still be seen ticking away is on Salisbury Cathedral in England. It is still going over 600 years after it was made in 1386, and chimes a bell on every hour.

THE OLDEST CENTRAL HEATING SYSTEM

The oldest central heating system dates back to Roman times. A 'hypocaust', which means 'heat from below', is an ancient heating system developed by Roman engineers.

The floor of a building was laid on top of small pillars, and then the open space below the floor was heated by a wood fire. As a result, warm air from the fire could circulate and heat the room, without filling it with smoke.

THE OLDEST SKYSCRAPER

The people of Chicago, USA, claim their city is the birthplace of the skyscraper. The Home Insurance Building was the first one built in the USA. When it was originally built, in 1885, the skyscraper had ten storeys and was 42 metres high. In 1890, two more floors were added.

The people of Chicago are wrong, however. The oldest skyscrapers in the world stand huddled together in the town of Shibam, Yemen. There are about 500 buildings made of mud, known as the 'Manhattan of the Desert'. They may not be as tall as Chicago's Home Insurance Building, but they are a lot older, having been built mainly in the 16th century.

THE OLDEST FLUSHING TOILET

Surprisingly, flushing toilets have been around since ancient times. One of the earliest examples was found at the palace of Knossos, Crete. It consisted of a seat over a drain and was flushed with water from a jug. Archaeologists have even found one in a 2,000-year-old royal tomb in China. Presumably it was for use in the afterlife. It was flushed by means of water carried in pipes. However, the king would have a long time to get hold of some toilet paper as it wasn't invented until about AD 100.

THE WORLD'S GREENEST

THE GREENEST COUNTRY

In 2012, Switzerland was labelled the world's greenest country, thanks to its strict laws on protecting air quality and its ecosystems.

China now leads the way in wind power, producing more than 26% of the world's wind energy. The world's biggest off-shore wind farm opened in 2012 off the coast of Cumbria, in the UK. It can generate enough electricity for 320,000 homes.

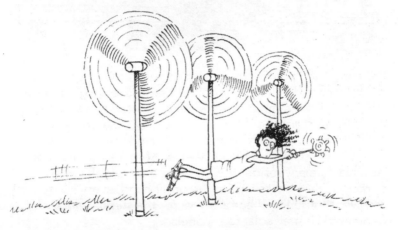

THE GREENEST BUILDING

According to the United States Green Building Council, one of the greenest buildings in the world is the Phipps Conservatory and Botanical Gardens' new Centre for Sustainable Landscapes (CSL) in Pittsburgh, USA, which opened in spring 2012. The building uses 80 per cent less energy than a comparable conventional building. Water is captured, treated and reused, and the building is heated by a combination of solar, photovoltaic, geothermal and wind energy.

THE GREENEST CITY

Freiburg is a city in Germany, and its severe building regulations and strict control of residents' lives might not suit everyone. For example, people are permitted to own cars, but they must pay a one-off charge of 18,000 euros (about £14,500) and a monthly rent to park them in the community car park, which is a fair distance away from their apartments. As a result, many residents who own cars avoid this charge by parking in the next town. On the other hand, every household receives thousands of euros a year for the surplus electricity generated by their solar roof panels.

The average house in Germany and Britain wastes about 220 kilowatts of electricity a year for every square metre of floor space. In Freiburg there are apartments that waste just 15 kilowatts. The apartments have wall insulation up to 30 centimetres thick and triple-glazed windows. Warm air flowing out of the house is also used to heat fresh, cooler air coming in. The apartments are heated by the warmth provided by the people who live there, by cooking and lighting. It is claimed that an entire apartment could be heated by only 30 candles.

THE GREATEST MEDICAL DISCOVERIES

The pioneers of medicine had to fight religious prejudices and ridicule from fellow physicians – so they had to be tough and not squeamish!

THE FIRST DOCTOR

Imhotep is thought to have been the first physician and surgeon in history to be known by name (see page 28). He was chief priest and first minister to King Djoser of Egypt. He wrote about many diseases and their treatments. Imhotep was worshipped for hundreds of years after he died as the god of medicine in Egypt and Ancient Greece.

THE FIRST ANATOMIST

Andreas Vesalius was born in Belgium in 1514. As a boy, he hung out at the local gallows, where executed prisoners were left to hang until they rotted away. His fascination with decomposing bodies led  to him writing *On the Structure of the Human Body*. This textbook transformed the study of human anatomy, as it was the first work to be based on actual observations of dissected human bodies.

THE FIRST ANTIBIOTICS

Ancient Egyptians used mouldy bread to prevent wounds becoming infected. This is not as strange an idea as it sounds. In 1928, Scottish Professor Alexander Fleming was clearing out his laboratory when he noticed a dish of bacteria had become contaminated by a mould called Penicillium notatum. He observed that the bacteria had been killed where they had come into contact with the mould. After refinement, the mould became the first antibiotic wonder-drug, now known as 'penicillin'.

THE FIRST HUMAN HEART TRANSPLANT

The first human heart transplant was performed by Dr Christiaan Barnard and a team of 20 surgeons in South Africa on the 3rd of December 1967. Though heart transplants are relatively common operations today, at the time it was an incredibly risky procedure. The man who received the heart was a grocer who was going to die if left untreated. He only lived for 18 days after the operation, because the drugs he was given to prevent him rejecting his donor heart made him vulnerable to infection.

Dr Barnard continued to perform transplant operations and was increasingly successful. By the end of the 1970s, his patients had a good chance of surviving for several years with their new hearts.

THE FIRST VACCINE

A milkmaid and a cow named Blossom started a chain of events that led an English country doctor, Edward Jenner, to one of the greatest medical discoveries of all time.

Jenner had heard an old-wives' tale that claimed milkmaids never got smallpox. Smallpox was a terrible disease that caused death in many sufferers and terrible disfigurement in those who survived it. Jenner knew that milkmaids often got a mild disease called cowpox, but those that did never caught smallpox. In 1796, when Sarah, a local milkmaid, developed cowpox blisters, Jenner took some pus and scratched it into the skin of a boy, named James Phipps. Two months later he did the same with the smallpox virus, but James didn't develop the disease. This process, called vaccination, has protected people against a range of diseases ever since.

THE FIRST ANTISEPTICS

In the 1800s, standards of hygiene in operating theatres were so bad that to be taken to hospital was almost a death sentence. An English surgeon named Joseph Lister observed that almost half of the patients on whom he performed amputations died of dreadful infections. Lister developed a system of cleaning everything that came into contact with a patient's wounds. In 1865, he used an 'antiseptic' called carbolic acid in the treatment of a boy's leg wound. He was able to successfully prove that this method destroyed germs and greatly reduced infection.

THE STUPIDEST SCIENCE

THE MOST BRAINLESS EXPERIMENT

Scientists at the Institute for Animal Health in Edinburgh, Scotland, worried that BSE, commonly known as 'mad cow disease', might pass to sheep. They began a major study of sheep's brains. When, after five years, they had made no progress, they feared the samples they were studying may have been contaminated by cow brain material. Sure enough, tests confirmed the brains they had been studying, which they thought were sheep's brains, were actually cows' brains all along.

THE NEWEST FOSSIL

In 1912, the world was excited by the discovery of a skull that seemed to be the 'missing link' between apes and our early ancestors. The fossilised remains became known as the 'Piltdown Man' and were exhibited in the National History Museum, London, for 40 years. In 1953, however, the fossils were revealed to be part of a hoax. Tests showed the jawbone belonged to an orang-utan. There was also a question raised about the prehistoric cricket bat that had been found with the skull.

THE WORLD'S BIGGEST OOPS!

The Hubble Space Telescope has proved to be one of the biggest science successes ever, but for a time after its launch in 1990, it didn't work. A programmer had confused centimetres and inches in his calculations meaning the curve of the telescope's mirror was out, so pictures were blurred. It took hundreds of millions of pound to put his error right.

THE MOST DESTRUCTIVE INVENTOR

Thomas Midgely, Jr made three significant inventions, all of which proved to be very destructive. The first was Freon, a gas used in refrigerators that has been shown to destroy the ozone layer, which is found high up in the Earth's atmosphere and absorbs harmful rays from the Sun. Freon is now banned. He developed CFCs, a group of chemical compounds that were subsequently used in aerosol sprays. CFCs are also banned because they destroy the ozone layer. Thirdly, Midgely discovered that a chemical compound called 'tetraethyl', which comes from lead, prevents something called 'engine knock' in cars. Later, lead was banned as a petrol additive in many countries, because it's poisonous. Sadly, Midgely contracted polio and lost the use of his legs. He died in 1944, when he accidentally strangled himself with a contraption he invented to get himself out of bed.

THE SMELLIEST MAN-MADE CHEMICALS

It is hard to believe, but scientists have worked hard to create some of the worst smells in the world. More pungent than the petals of the titan arum (see page 207) and stinkier than the anal glands of a skunk (see page 194) is a group of man-made chemicals called 'thiols'.

Man-made thiols are added to some substances to make them smell. Natural gas used to heat homes and cook food has no smell. This can be dangerous if there is a gas leak and no one is able to detect it. So gas companies add one of the thiols to gas to alert everyone to the presence of explosive gas.

THE LARGEST AND SMALLEST COUNTRIES

THE LARGEST COUNTRY

Russia (Russian Federation) covers 17 million square kilometres, an eighth of the Earth's total land area. It's by far the biggest country in the world.

There are 9 time zones across the country. There used to be 11, but in 2010, two were cut to improve communication between time zones, and to improve rail, bus and air services. Even so, when it is 9 o'clock in the morning in Kaliningrad, in the west, it is already 6 o'clock in the evening in the east, in Provideniya.

Around 142 million people live in Russia, but due to its massive size, there's not much of a squeeze – about 9 people per square kilometre.

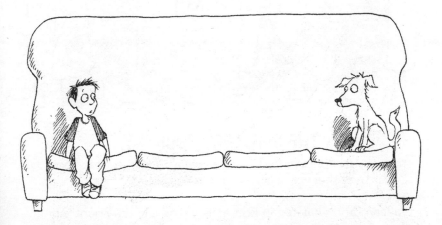

Russia doesn't, however, hold the title of the largest country by population. This title belongs to China – which on the 18th of July 2008, was said to have a population of over 1.3 billion people. This gave China almost 20 per cent of the total population of the planet (the planet's population is always growing, but is currently just over 7 billion).

However, by 2040, experts predict India's population will be 1.68 billion, whereas China's will be only 1.45 billion in the same year.

THE SMALLEST COUNTRY

You would expect to find cities inside a country, but Vatican City is the other way around – it is a tiny country inside a city.

Vatican City is located in Rome, Italy. The city is a country in its own right – it mints its own coins, prints its own stamps and has its own national anthem and flag. It issues its own passports and car number plates even though it has no major roads for the cars to drive on. The Pope, who is the leader of the Roman Catholic Church, lives in Vatican City and he is protected by guards who wear fancy, traditional uniforms.

This entire country covers a total of 44 hectares, which is less than half a square kilometre, and it has only 829 citizens.

THE LARGEST CITY

Tokyo, Japan, is home to over 34 million people, making it the largest city in the world. The number of people living in the city is over half the total number of people living in the whole of the United Kingdom. Approximately 4,750 people live in every square kilometre of Tokyo.

THE MOST CROWDED CITY

Tokyo may sound crowded, but not as much as Manila, capital of the Philippines. Here, there are an estimated 43,079 people per square kilometre, making Manila the most crowded city in the world. Compare this to London, for example – with only 4,900 people per square kilometre.

AMAZING AND MAN-MADE

THE TALLEST BUILDING

On the 7th of April 2008, the Burj Khalifa became the world's tallest residential building – and it was still growing. Its outer structure was completed in October 2009, with a final height of 828 metres, much taller than the previous record-holder (Taipei 101, a mere 509.2 metres high).

The Burj Khalifa is built in a spiral shape, a bit like a corkscrew. The tip of the spire at the top of the hotel can be seen 95 kilometres away. The temperature in Dubai can reach as high as 47°C, so the outside of the building is covered with special steel panels that look like silvery glass. These reflect the Sun's heat and keep the building cooler.

THE HIGHEST RAILWAY

If you were to take the train that runs from China's capital city, Beijing, to Tibet's capital, Llasa, you would be travelling on the highest railway in the world. The trip takes 48 hours, and the 1,140-kilometre-long track climbs to 5,000 metres above sea level at its highest point.

Even though extra oxygen is pumped into the train during the ride, many passengers need to lie-down or wear oxygen masks at the highest point in the journey, because of altitude sickness and headaches.

THE HIGHEST ROAD BRIDGE

The Millau bridge, in the Massif Central mountains in France, towers more than 300 metres above the river Tarn. This beautiful bridge was built to divert cars around the town of Millau, to stop traffic jams. Unfortunately, the town now suffers more traffic jams as a result of the huge number of people coming to see the world's highest road bridge.

THE HIGHEST FLIGHT BY AN AIRCRAFT

The SR-71 Blackbird is a record-breaking manned aircraft. The jet is about 32 metres long, with a wingspan of nearly 17 metres. It can travel at a speed of over 3,540 kilometres an hour which is over three times the speed of sound. It can reach heights of up to 26 kilometres above ground level.

In 2001, an unmanned aircraft called Helios (shown below) soared to a height of 29.5 kilometres after it took off from an airbase in Hawaii. Helios is much slower than the SR-71 Blackbird. Its top speed is about 322 kilometres per hour. It runs on batteries charged by solar cells on its wings and is radio-controlled from the ground.

Rocket planes can fly even higher – so high that they reach the verge of outer space. In 2004, a rocket plane called SpaceShipOne flew to a record-breaking height of 112 kilometres above the Earth's surface. The SpaceShipOne rocket plane was piloted by a man named Brian Binnie.

THE MOST MISLEADING LEADERS

THE FIRST AND LAST FEMALE POPE

The Pope is head of the Catholic Church and he is always a man. Over 1,000 years ago, however, legend has it that there was a female pope, known as Pope Joan.

A document written in the 13th century claimed that in 855, Johannes Angelicus became pope and reigned for nearly three years. Johannes was in fact Joan or Joanna, an English woman who had disguised herself as a man. Her disguise was so convincing that no one realised she was a woman.

The story goes that while she was pope, Joan got pregnant. One day, during a procession from St Peter's in Rome, she gave birth to a child. On discovering that their revered pope was actually an unmarried woman, it is said that the crowd were so angry they killed her.

Whether or not Pope Joan ever existed, or was even a woman, may never be known. The first real attempt to prove that she didn't exist was written in 1647, long after she was supposed to have died.

DON'T YOU LIKE THE COLOUR?

THE FIRST FEMALE PHARAOH

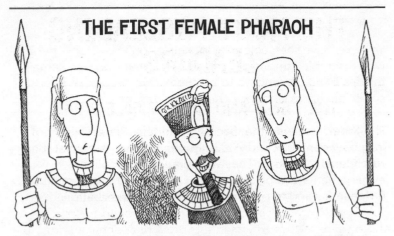

In 1473 BC, Hatshepsut became not only the first woman to rule in Egypt, but also the only female pharaoh to pretend to be a man.

Hatshepsut married her half brother, Thutmose II. They had no sons, only a daughter. So when he died in 1479 BC, the throne passed to his son, Thutmose III, born to another of his wives. As Thutmose III was very young, Hatshepsut co-ruled with him, and eventually had herself crowned king.

After taking the title of pharaoh, Hatshepsut insisted on having herself shown as a man in pictures. She dropped the female ending to her name and became 'His Majesty Hatshepsu', and started wearing a male tunic and headdress. She even wore a false beard.

Hatshepsut ruled successfully for 21 years, until she died in 1458 BC. In 1903, when archeologist Howard Carter (see page 75) was excavating in the Valley of the Kings in Egypt, he found an unmarked tomb that contained the mummified body of a female. A box of preserved organs was found close by, among which was a broken tooth. This broken tooth fitted perfectly into a gap in the jaw of the mummified female. DNA tests proved that the mummy was the body of the female pharaoh, Hatshepsut.

THE BEST LOOKALIKES

You may have seen celebrity lookalikes on television – people who resemble famous people so much that they can actually make a living pretending to be them. But there have been some lookalikes who took this a step further.

It is widely believed that Saddam Hussein, the president of Iraq between 1979 and 2003, employed a team of lookalikes to pretend to be him. They would appear at political engagements and on television. Hussein did this to confuse his enemies and to protect himself from assassination.

THE MOST MISLEADING HEROINE

Joan of Arc is a national heroine of France, but during her lifetime many people thought she was a hero. Joan was born in 1412, when France was at war with England. She claimed the voices of saints had told her to rid France of the enemy. So, she dressed like a male soldier to lead the French army.

It is said that when Joan was shot in the chest with an arrow during a battle, she pulled it out and continued fighting. When imprisoned, she was determined to escape and leapt from a castle tower, falling unconscious into the moat. Later, Joan was accused of witchcraft and burned to death at the stake in 1431.

THE MOST MISLEADING PHOTOGRAPHS

People say that the camera never lies – well once upon a time it did. From 1922 to 1991, the country now known as Russia was grouped together with a number of other countries and called the Soviet Union. The Soviet Union was big and powerful, with a government many other countries around the world didn't like. This made the Soviet Union feel threatened, and the people who ruled the country were scared of being overthrown. They became very secretive and suspicious, both of the outside world and of people within their own country. Anyone who was considered a traitor was dealt with very harshly – sent to a hard-labour camp or executed. Some people just disappeared in the middle of the night, with no official reason being given for where they had gone.

As a result, people tried to alter history to exaggerate their importance. Some had themselves added to photographs of events at which they had not been present. One man who did this more than any other was Josef Stalin. He ruled the Soviet Union for almost a quarter of a century, until his death in 1953. Stalin did everything he could to make himself look like the rightful ruler. He even forged photographs of himself standing alongside the previous leader, Lenin. Stalin was vain enough to make himself look taller and hopefully more powerful in the fake pictures. Stalin also used photographs to make his rivals look bad, having them removed from photographs or erased from history altogether.

THE UNLUCKIEST LEADERS

THE SHORTEST TERM FOR A US PRESIDENT

William Henry Harrison worked hard for 50 years to become President of the USA. On the day he took office in 1841, he caught a cold. The cold turned into pneumonia and he died less than a month later, becoming the first president to die in office and serve the shortest time in power.

THE LEADER MOST STABBED IN THE BACK

Being in charge of all that would become the Roman Empire might sound brilliant, but it didn't do much good for Julius Caesar. After joining the Roman Army, Caesar quickly moved up through the ranks, winning a civil war and extending the powers of Rome throughout the globe.

By 46 BC, his successes on the battlefield led him to be elected as the sole ruler of Rome. Returning from the battlefield to look after his people, Caesar attempted to make radical changes in the way Rome was governed. He was so powerful that he could pick and choose which politicians could stay to advise him and sack the ones that didn't agree with him.

Caesar's supposed friends and closest advisors – 60 politicians in total – thought that the power had gone to Caesar's head and that he must be stopped in order to save Rome. They plotted to kill him and on the 15th of March 44 BC, the members of the Senate (the governors of Rome) stabbed him with knives that they had hidden under their togas.

Reportedly, they all wanted to take part in the murder, each of them wishing to take a stab at the all-powerful Julius Caesar. Caesar was stabbed many times before he died.

THE UNLUCKIEST QUEEN

Lady Jane Grey was Queen of England for just nine days before she was imprisoned in the Tower of London and later beheaded. When Henry VIII died, his niece Jane was named heir to the throne, but only if his children Edward, Mary and Elizabeth, died first.

Edward became king in 1547, and ruled for six years. On his deathbed he declared his wish to leave the throne to Jane, instead of his half-sister, Mary. So in July 1553, at the age of 15, Jane became Queen of England.

Unsurprisingly, Mary was furious and claimed the throne for herself. Jane was accused of treason, imprisoned and forced to give up her crown. On the day of her execution in 1554, Jane protested she had not wanted to become queen and had only been doing as she was told.

THE MOST HATED QUEEN

Marie Antoinette was only 15 when she married King Louis XVI of France in 1770. She enjoyed fabulous luxury at the Palace of Versailles, near Paris, France. Her incredible spending sprees added to the country's vast debts. In contrast, the ordinary people of France were suffering terrible poverty. Marie Antoinette failed to understand their misery and many began to hate her. For a long time, people believed that she even said, 'Let them eat cake!' when she heard the people had no bread, but this is a myth.

When revolution broke out in 1789, a mob forced Marie Antoinette, her husband and children, out of the palace. The family attempted to escape, but were captured. The king was overthrown in 1792, and imprisoned. In prison, Marie Antoinette was cruelly treated. Her children were taken from her and the head of her best friend Princess de Lambelle was paraded on a spike in front of her. In 1793, aged 37 years old, Marie Antoinette was sent to the guillotine and beheaded.

FANTASTIC FLAGS

THE MOST CHANGING FLAG

Before 1776, the USA was made up of 13 colonies and was ruled by the British. The British flag was the national flag. Many people in the USA were not happy under British rule and wanted to be free. They fought the British and declared their independence in 1776.

In 1777, a new American flag was approved – the 'Stars and Stripes'. It was first flown during a battle with the English at Fort McHenry. The Americans wanted the flag to be big and bold enough for the British to see at a distance. A woman called Mary Young Pickersgill made the first flag.

She used 366 metres of wool cloth and added 13 stars and stripes to represent the 13 original colonies, or states, that made up the USA. The colours of the flag were red, white and blue – red for courage, white for purity and blue for loyalty. When it was finished the flag was raised above the fort for all to see. Since then, the flag has changed 27 times as new states joined the Union. There are now 50 states and 50 stars on the flag. The last two stars were added in 1959, when Alaska and Hawaii became part of the USA. The number of stripes has remained 13.

The biggest ever national flag was unfurled for the first time in Lebanon in October 2010. The flag covered a total area of 65,975 square metres and weighed a massive 6 tonnes. It dwarfs the previous largest ever flag, which was made in Morocco and covered a relatively paltry 60,000 square metres.

THE SMALLEST FLAG

Scientists at the University of Texas in Dallas, USA, have created a tiny American flag complete with all 50 stars and 13 stripes. It is so small that it cannot get into the record books, because there's no way for the adjudicators to see it and verify it exists!

The students who created this minute flag said they did it to demonstrate just how small they can make things nowadays using what is called 'nanotechnology'. Nanotechnology means 'really small' technology.

THE MOST USEFUL FLAGS

In the time before radio communication and mobile phones, issuing urgent orders within the navy was very difficult. It was fine to shout loud enough for the seamen on your own ship to hear, but communicating with other ships while under attack was almost impossible.

In 1800, Sir Home Riggs Popham, a rear admiral, came up with a clever way of signalling to other ships. He devised a code which involved hoisting flags, each with a differently coloured design. The code was known as the Telegraphic Signals of Marine Vocabulary.

THE TALLEST FLAGPOLE TOPPLED BY BIRDS

The tallest flagpole to be toppled by birds is a massive wooden structure that originally stood in Kew Gardens in London, England. When it was first constructed in 1959, the pole measured 69 metres tall, which made it the world's tallest flagpole at the time. Since then it has been shortened a number of times to make it safe. Then, in August 2007, the pole was taken down because it had become too dangerous to raise a flag. Woodpeckers had damaged the pole making it unsafe.

Today, the tallest flagpoles don't have this problem.

They are made of metal, which would give a curious woodpecker a heck of a headache.

TIMBER!

THE MOST TREACHEROUS SPIES AND TRAITORS

THE MOST BEAUTIFUL SPY

Mata Hari was executed by firing squad in France in 1917, for being a double agent. At the time, France and Germany were fighting each other in the First World War.

Mata Hari was a very beautiful woman and had many love affairs – some with French and German officers. When she was arrested, she was accused of passing French military secrets to the Germans. She was charged with treason and sentenced to death by firing squad. One report says that Mata Hari refused to wear a blindfold, and, dressed in her best suit and hat, she faced her executioners with a smile.

Some say Mata Hari was not a spy at all, but just a woman who fell in love with the wrong men. There has never been any evidence that Mata Hari passed on any specific information.

The legend of this mysterious and beautiful spy has led to Mata Hari being portrayed in many films and even a video game. Most famously, she was played in a movie by an actress named Greta Garbo.

THE MOST TREACHEROUS TEAM

Today, university is a place to study, try out new hobbies and join different clubs and societies. In the 1930s, however, the University of Cambridge, England, was a place where you could go to become a spy.

Five friends at Cambridge University – Kim Philby, Guy Burgess, Anthony Blunt, Donald Maclean and John Cairncross – did just that. They became secret agents, working for the Soviet Union. They are known as the 'Cambridge Spy Ring'.

After university, the five men went to work for the British Government and the secret service. They acted as 'double agents' – they appeared to work for British intelligence, but really they were Soviet intelligence operatives. In the 1940s and 1950s, there was a great deal of rivalry between the Soviet Union, Britain and America. From their positions of trust, the members of the spy ring were able to send important secret information to the Soviet Union, including information about a new weapon called the 'atomic bomb' and about spies working against the Russians.

From the 1950s onwards, members of the spy ring were caught and revealed as double agents. Kim Philby, Guy Burgess and Donald Maclean fled England. Anthony Blunt claimed he stopped working as a spy in 1945, but his past came to light in 1979. John Cairncross managed to keep his true identity secret until 1990.

THE MOST FAMOUS FAILED PLOT

A 'traitor' is someone who is disloyal and betrays their country. A man named Guy Fawkes was arrested as a traitor on the 4th of November 1605, when he was caught red-handed beneath the Houses of Parliament in London guarding 36 barrels of gunpowder. Fawkes and his fellow conspirators had stored the barrels there in an attempt to blow up the building and kill King James I.

When James became King of England and Scotland after the death of Elizabeth I, he continued her policy of attacking people who followed the Catholic faith. Fawkes and his group wanted to show their anger at this.

Luckily for King James and the politicians of the time, the plot failed. James' men found out about the plan and arrested Fawkes. He was tortured horribly and eventually gave up the names of his fellow conspirators. They were arrested and executed along with Fawkes.

To this day, when Queen Elizabeth II enters the Houses of Parliament for a ceremony called the 'State Opening of Parliament', the cellars underneath the building are searched to make sure everything is safe.

Every year on the 5th of November, the British celebrate Bonfire Night, to mark the day that King James was saved. Fireworks are lit and a stuffed dummy, known as a 'guy' after Mr Fawkes, is placed on a bonfire.

THE MOST INGENIOUS SPYWARE

THE ENIGMA MACHINE

In Germany, in 1918, a man called Arthur Scherbius designed a machine that looked like a typewriter, but was far more interesting. It was used to code and decode messages and was called the Enigma machine. It was most famously used during the Second World War, and worked by substituting the letters typed in an original message with different letters. It used a complex series of rotating disks and electrical connections to make coded messages that were incredibly difficult to crack.

THE MOST TECHNOLOGICALLY ADVANCED ROCK

In 2006, Russia's state security service, known as the FSB, accused British diplomats in Moscow of spying. It was reported that a fake rock had been found on the outskirts of Moscow. The light-brown rock greatly concerned the FSB, who claimed it was hollow and contained an electronic transmitter used to download data onto the palm-top computers of people working for the British secret service. They said that footage from a hidden camera appeared to show people approaching the rock regularly.

THE MOST LETHAL UMBRELLA

In 1978, Georgi Markov, a Bulgarian journalist working for the BBC World Service, died as he waited at a bus stop. At his autopsy – the examination of the body – a minute pellet containing traces of the poison ricin was found embedded in his leg. It is thought that an umbrella was used to conceal a mechanism that injected the poison and had been operated by an agent working for either the Bulgarian government or for the Soviet Union's security agency, known as the KGB. Markov had been strongly against the Bulgarian government at the time and its agents may have wanted to silence him.

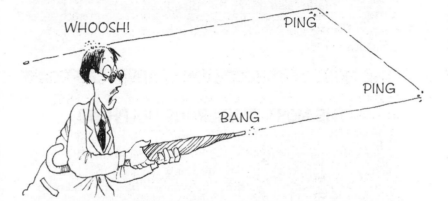

THE MOST DARING DESIGNS

Illustrations of women's fashion wouldn't be the first place you would look for secret messages. However, that is exactly where German spies operating in the UK hid some of their messages. Illustrations containing secret information were sent back to 'spy masters' in Germany. There, they would be studied and the messages decoded. One drawing of three models wearing the latest fashions showed stitches around the hem that formed a message in Morse code, which uses dots and dashes. The code signalled 'Heavy reinforcements for the enemy expected hourly'.

THE MOST MISLEADING FOOTPRINTS

In the Far East, during the Second World War, British soldiers had a problem. Local people tended to go about barefoot and the soldiers, who wore big army boots, created footprints that were instantly recognisable. On occasion, this gave away their location to the enemy, so to solve the problem, soldiers were issued with ingenious 'footprint sandals'.

These fake feet, with clever bare-foot soles, made false tracks that disguised each step the soldiers took.

THE MOST DANGEROUS DOLPHINS

In 2003, the US military began a secret programme of underwater mine detection and enemy elimination. The military developed a sophisticated new weapon that had a built-in 'echolocation' system. The weapon had the ability to identify and destroy underwater intruders and then return to base. What were these incredible new pieces of spyware? Dolphins – dolphins with guns. These amazing mammals were trained to protect US military ships by firing toxic darts at enemy divers. The darts were carried on a special harness the dolphins were fitted with.

Unfortunately, there was a downside to the release of these aquatic avengers. In 2005, a hurricane, named hurricane Katrina, caused widespread damage. This damage included flooding the compound in which the dolphins were kept, setting them free. It is rumoured that the dolphins had their weapon harnesses on, and some people feared that they could target innocent swimmers.

THE LEAST CRYPTIC CODE

In wartime, communication between army units or ships at sea and command headquarters is crucial. Encoding messages to disguise their content from the enemy takes time, and delays can cost lives. In 1942, a civilian named Philip Johnston told the allied forces he knew a simple way to communicate over phone lines or radio broadcasts. He said that although the enemy in Germany and Japan would be able to hear everything that was said, they wouldn't be able to understand the messages. His method didn't involve a code at all.

Johnston grew up with the Navajo, a tribe of Native North Americans, and spoke their language fluently. Apart from him and the Navajo themselves, only a handful of people in the world knew the language. He was certain that none of the enemy would understand it. Secret information could be spoken about freely with a Navajo speaker at each end of the line. Normal speech is much faster than Morse code or encryption – putting text into code – so the plan worked brilliantly. Things that the Navajo had no words for such as 'aircraft carrier,' were given substitute words, such as 'whale'. The 400 Navajo who took part in this important project are credited with saving hundreds of lives. They were known as the Navajo Code Talkers.

THE GREATEST ESCAPES

THE MOST DETERMINED QUEEN

During a rebellion between the Scottish nobles in 1567, Mary Queen of Scots was imprisoned on an island off the coast of Scotland, in a castle called Lochleven. Mary was very brave and although she was kept under strict guard, she was determined to escape. She had to wait a year for the right moment. When this came, she disguised herself as a local washerwoman, and escaped to the mainland by boat. Unfortunately, the man hired to row her, noticed she had the soft white hands of a lady. A washerwoman would have had rough, red hands. The man turned Mary over to her captors and she was taken back to the castle.

Mary tried to escape again with the help of a boy, known as Wee Willie, whom she had befriended. He organised a party on the island to distract the attention of the guards. Meanwhile, Mary made her escape dressed as a servant. This time she was successful. She was rowed from the castle to the mainland. There, a horse stolen from her captor's stables was waiting for her.

THE GREAT ESCAPE

On the 24th of March 1944, during the Second World War, 76 men escaped from Stalag Luft III, a German prisoner-of-war camp for captured airmen near the town of Zagan, Poland. On a moonless night, they were led to freedom by Squadron Leader Roger Bushell – code named Big X. He and his committee had planned for over 250 men to escape through three tunnels called 'Tom', 'Dick' and 'Harry'.

The tunnels were dug into the sand below the huts in which the prisoners were kept. Sand collapses easily, so the tunnels were supported with boards taken from the men's beds. Milk tins were used to make ventilation pipes and there was even an underground railway used to shift sand along and out of the tunnel.

Getting rid of all the sand the prisoners dug out was difficult. Guards, nicknamed 'ferrets' by the prisoners, were always on the lookout for signs of escape, and huge piles of sand would be a massive giveaway. Prisoners called 'penguins' hid the sand in long tubes made from old towels and slipped the tubes down the legs of their trousers. They got rid of the sand by emptying it out while standing near people working in the prison gardens. The gardeners then covered it up quickly.

For the escape, tailors made clothes from blankets and old uniforms so that the escapees could blend in with the civilian population. The tunnel named 'Dick' had to be abandoned as an escape route when a new compound was built on top of the place where the tunnel came to the surface. Tunnel 'Tom' was discovered during the summer of 1943, so all the effort went into 'Harry'.

Of the 76 men who escaped, only three made it to safety – 50 were shot under the direct order of Adolf Hitler, in order to discourage future escapes, and 23 were sent back to prison camps. Even though so few got to safety, this escape was one of the greatest escapes of all time.

THE BEST HIDING PLACES

THE BEST PLACES TO HIDE
IN THE SECOND WORLD WAR

During the Second World War, Casper Ten Boom's house in Haarlem, Holland, became a hiding place for people persecuted by the Nazis. Between 1943 and 1944, Casper and his daughters, Corrie and Betsie, had up to seven people hiding there every day.

One of the hiding places in the house was a dark, cupboard-like room behind a false wall in Corrie's bedroom. The room was so well hidden that even when the house was searched it wasn't found. Once, when the house was being searched, six people hid in this room. They stayed there for 47 hours, without food or water, not making a sound, before they could be moved to another 'safe house'. The Ten Boom family were not so lucky; they were caught and imprisoned. Later in the war, Corrie and Betsie were sent to a concentration camp, where many people were killed. Only Corrie survived. She was honoured for her bravery.

Anne Frank hid from the Nazis with her family in a house in Amsterdam, Holland, until they were discovered and sent to a concentration camp, where Anne died. Her story is famous thanks to her diary, which became a bestseller after the war.

THE MOST SECRET RAILROAD

The Underground Railroad was neither underground nor a railroad. It was the name given to an escape route for African slaves travelling north from the southern states of America in the 1800s. It was called 'underground' because it was kept very secret. No information was ever written down and details of the route were passed on only by word of mouth.

The slaves who used the Underground Railroad were escaping to freedom. They had been born into slavery after their ancestors had been taken from their homes in West Africa to work on the plantations in North America. Working conditions were hard, and slaves had no rights or freedom. They could be bought or sold and separated from their families at any time. They could be beaten and even killed by their owners.

The Railroad's network of secret routes were referred to as 'lines', which people only travelled on at night, often on foot. The slaves, known as 'freight', were guided by 'conductors'. During the day they rested in hiding places called 'stations' and were looked after by people called 'station masters'. Some reports say that up to 100,000 slaves escaped in this way, travelling to Canada, which was beyond the reach of slave hunters.

THE MOST SECRET TUNNELS

During the 1960s, the people of South Vietnam, with the help of the Americans, were fighting the people of North Vietnam. It was a long and bitter conflict. A guerrilla force fighting for the North Vietnamese, known as the Viet Cong, built the Cu Chi tunnels near Saigon, where they lived and planned their battles. Over 250 kilometres of passageways crisscrossed the countryside. Some of the passages were like underground villages, containing schools, hospitals and kitchens. The tunnel entrances, exits and ventilation pipes were ingeniously disguised and despite the Americans' superior technology, the tunnels made a big difference to the outcome of the war, in which South Vietnam was eventually defeated.

THE BEST HIDING PLACE FOR A KING

Not far from the English border in Dumfriesshire, Scotland, are some cliffs that rise 9 metres above a river called Kirtle Water. Deep inside these cliffs is a cave that is very difficult to find. There is a footpath to it now, but before 1927, you could only reach it by being lowered on a rope and swinging, like Tarzan, through the entrance.

Legend has it that in 1306, this cave was the hiding place of Robert the Bruce, the King of Scotland. He is said to have used the cave to hide from English soldiers who were trying to kill him. While he was hiding in the cave he had plenty of time to think about how best to defeat the English in battle. The story tells how Robert watched a spider weaving its web in the entrance of the cave. Though the web was destroyed many times, the spider kept rebuilding it. Inspired by the spider's determination and refusal to give up, Robert decided to keep fighting. Sure enough, his army beat the English at the Battle of Bannockburn in the year 1314.

THE BEST HIDING PLACE FOR A HIGHWAYMAN

A highwayman was a robber who would wait by a roadside to ambush passing travellers. They were feared greatly because they would demand people's valuables, in return for sparing their lives. In the 18th century a former cattle thief named Dick Turpin became the most famous highwayman of all.

Turpin was a cruel man who often tortured travellers to make them hand over their belongings. When he held up a stagecoach with the famous words, 'Your money or your life' – he really meant it!

In 1735, Dick Turpin joined forces with another highwayman known as Captain Tom King. They had a hiding place deep in the heart of Epping Forest in England. Their hiding place was a cave large enough to fit five men and hidden from the road by large bushes and branches. From it, they could lie in wait for passers-by. It is said that the cave was discovered in 1737 after a servant spotted Turpin in the entrance.

Turpin is said to have killed Tom King by accident while shooting at a police constable. But he had more luck when trying to escape capture, and his career as a highwayman lasted nearly five years. In that time he became legendary, as did the reward on his head. Turpin was finally caught and hanged in 1739.

DOESN'T IT SUIT ME?

THE DUMBEST CRIMINALS

THE SLOWEST CAR CHASE

A dairy farmer was out milking cows when a neighbour told him there was someone in his house. He ran back to find the front door smashed open and his children locked in the bathroom, but the intruder had already left.

The farmer drove off in his car to chase the villain. It was pouring with rain, but a few kilometres down the road he spotted the bizarre getaway vehicle. The farmer was astonished to see that the burglar had chosen to escape using a wheelbarrow to carry the stolen belongings! What's more strange is that the cheeky chap pushing it also tried to thumb a lift from the farmer, but he refused, preferring to follow from a safe distance.

The farmer had to phone the police six times before they believed him. So the seriously slow chase continued for a couple of hours until eventually, the police finally arrived and arrested the exhausted criminal for burglary.

THE WORLD'S POOREST BUSINESS PLAN

In April 2008, 21-year-old Charles Ray Fuller was arrested for attempted fraud. Charles had wanted to start a record company. He planned to finance his new company with a forged cheque. He took this cheque to a branch of the Chase Bank in Fort Worth, Texas, USA. It was written out to 'Fuller Comp & Entertainment', his new company, and was signed by someone called 'Paula Prettyman'.

The people at the bank became very suspicious. The cheque was for 360 billion dollars, roughly three times the value of all of the gold held by the USA in Fort Knox (the place where most of the USA's gold is kept). The bank spoke to Paula Prettyman. She turned out to be the mother of Fuller's girlfriend. She said she hadn't signed the cheque and she didn't have 360 billion dollars, anyway. Fuller was arrested.

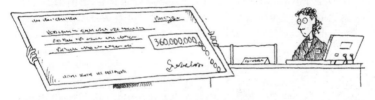

THE LEAST LIKELY PERSON TO SUCCEED IN CRIME

A man was charged with robbing a jewellery store in Liège, Belgium. He made up several stories, suggesting he was elsewhere at the time, but the police exposed them all as untrue. Finally, the man swore he could not have been at the jewellery store, because he had been breaking into a school that day.

The police arrested the man and charged him not only with breaking into the school, but also for the additional crime of wasting police time.

THE HOTTEST PANTS

When the police arrived at the scene of a bank robbery in the USA, they had no difficulty picking out the suspect among a crowd of witnesses – a man whose trousers were on fire.

The flaming felon must have been new to bank robbery. He yelled 'This is a hold-down!', when someone more experienced in these things might say 'This is a hold-up!' As he was running away from the bank, stuffing wads of money out of sight into the waistband of his trousers, they exploded.

A security dye pack had gone off. These little explosive devices are designed to burst, spraying dye that can't be removed all over the money to make it unusable. The robber suffered burns and was sent to hospital.

It is said he walked in very slowly.

THE CRIMINAL WITH THE BIGGEST MOUTH

A man in Brazil had terrorised his neighbours with a gun. When the police arrived they found him barricaded in his own house. He refused to come out and threatened to shoot anyone who came in to get him.

The police surrounded the building and waited to see what the man did next. It was several hours before someone noticed that the gunman had somehow got out of his house. He was standing right behind the policemen, and shouting 'Come out with your hands up!' at the empty house.

THE SMALLEST
(BUT NOT-SO-STUPID) CRIMINAL

Police in Stockholm, Sweden, were stumped. There had been a number of thefts from luggage left in the holds of coaches. The doors to the holds were locked straight after passengers' loaded their luggage in, and only opened just before they took their bags at the end of the journeys. No one else touched the bags, yet thousands of pounds worth of belongings went missing over a period of months.

It was eventually discovered that one of the bags on each bus contained a little person, loaded into the hold by an accomplice. During the trip, the little person would get out, help himself from the other luggage, and be back in his own bag ready to be taken off at the other end. Police questioned every person 'of limited stature' with a criminal record – but to this day no one has been arrested.

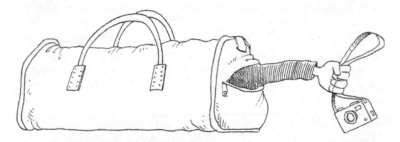

THE CHEEKIEST CRIMINAL

A man in Spain was arrested by police under suspicion of having carried out a series of bag-snatching offences. He loudly protested his innocence.

On the day that the suspect came to court to prove that the police had arrested the wrong man, he was wearing a particularly expensive suit. One of the people who had been a victim of the bag snatcher recognised the suit – it had been in the bag that was stolen from him.

THE SMARTEST LAW ENFORCER

THE BEST-DISGUISED DETECTIVE

If you go to Top Hat Terrace, a road in Leicester, England, you will see carvings of 16 different heads. All of the heads belong to the same man – Tanky Smith – Leicester's first private detective. Tanky was renowned for being a master of disguise.

In the mid-1800s, Leicester was a lawless place, full of criminal gangs. In an attempt to go undercover and mingle with gang members in bars and inns, Tanky adopted many disguises. Sometimes he was a jockey, sometimes a priest or a bishop. Tanky's real name was Francis Smith. Working undercover with his partner Tommy Haynes, Smith got enough evidence to prosecute many of the worst criminals of his day and cleaned up the city.

THE SILLIEST LAWS

1. In Ohio, USA, it is illegal to get a fish drunk.
2. In the UK, it is an act of treason to position a postage stamp bearing a king's or queen's head upside down.
3. In Victoria, Australia, it is an offence to wear pink hotpants after midday on Sundays.
4. In Florida, USA, it is illegal for unmarried women to parachute on Sundays.
5. In England, drivers of black taxi cabs are required to ask all passengers if they have smallpox or the plague.
6. In China, you are not allowed to rescue anyone who is drowning because it is thought you are interfering with their fate.
7. In Switzerland, after 10pm, it is an offence for a man to pee standing up.
8. In California, USA, it is illegal to set a mousetrap without a hunting licence.
9. In the city of Joliet in Illinois, USA, a woman can be arrested for trying on more than six dresses in one shop.
10. In the UK any person found breaking a boiled egg at the sharp end can be sentenced to 24 hours in the village stocks.

11. In France, it is illegal to name a pig Napoleon.

12. In Milan, Italy, there is a legal requirement to smile at all times, except at funerals or during hospital visits.

13. In Kentucky, USA, it is illegal to carry a concealed weapon that is more than 1.8 metres long.

14. Kissing on French railways is forbidden, and in Greece, if a man is caught kissing a woman the death penalty can be enforced.

15. In England, any boy under ten years old may not look at a naked shop dummy.

16. In Beijing, China, you could be fined if you stop your car at a pedestrian crossing to let someone cross the road.

17. In Alabama, USA, it is not lawful to flick snot into the wind.

18. In Chester, UK, it is legal to shoot a Welsh person with a bow and arrow, as long as the event occurs within the city walls and it is after midnight.

19. In Alabama, USA, it is illegal to drive a vehicle while blindfolded.

20. In Vermont, USA, women must get consent from their husbands before wearing false teeth.

THE GREATEST TREASURE

THE BEST REASON TO TIDY UNDER YOUR BED

Sometimes, great works of art turn up in unexpected places. In May 2008, a man called John Webber found out that he had something rather unexpected hidden under his bed. A battered metal container he had been given by his grandfather turned out to be a solid-gold cup that was over 2,000 years old and worth over £50,000. Mr Webber had shoved it under his bed in a shoe box 60 years earlier and had forgotten about it.

John Webber's grandfather was a 'rag-and-bone man', which meant he earned money riding around town in a cart picking up anything people didn't want anymore. One day he was given the cup and, thinking it was interesting but not worth anything, gave it to his grandson who used it for target practice.

The cup was only 14 centimetres tall and was decorated with two faces. Experts think that it might date back to the 3rd or 4th century BC and come from the Achaemenid Empire – an area based around what is now Iran and Libya. Mr Webber also had a golden spoon given to him by his grandfather which sold for £5,000.

THE MOST VALUABLE SHIPWRECK

There are a lot of secrets surrounding a ship code-named 'Black Swan', thought to be the most valuable wreck ever found. It is not clear exactly what ship it is or even where it was found.

The people who discovered it, in 2007, were from a professional treasure-hunting company called Odyssey Marine Exploration, based in Florida, USA. All the company will say is that the wreck was found somewhere in the Atlantic Ocean.

Over half a million 17th-century gold and silver coins, ornaments and tableware, weighing a total of 17 tonnes and worth an estimated £250 million, have already been recovered. Yet the wreck may contain even more treasure.

Countries are already arguing over the treasure. Spain and Portugal are both claiming a share. Spain says the wreck is one of their ships, which was bound for Cadiz from Peru, when it was sunk by the British navy in 1804. The Portuguese claim that as the ship was found off their coast it must be theirs. Peru also has a claim on the ship, believing the gold and silver was stolen from their ancestors by the Spanish.

THE MOST TREACHEROUS TREASURE

The most famous treasure-find of all time was the discovery of the tomb of the boy king, Tutankhamun, in the Valley of the Kings in Egypt. It was discovered in November 1922, by the archeologist Howard Carter and his team. It was the first tomb of an Egyptian pharaoh to be discovered that had lain undisturbed by robbers since his death 3,000 years ago.

Later, when Howard Carter was asked by journalists what he could see when he first opened the tomb, he replied, 'Wonderful things!' Among the items discovered were gold jewellery and precious stones and a magnificent solid-gold face-mask of Tutankhamun himself. There were also the toys he had played with as a child, including a painting set and toy soldiers. There was even a supply of socks and clean underwear for the pharaoh to wear in the afterlife.

Although all of these treasures were indisputably wonderful, many people believed they were also cursed. They believed that in removing the items from the tomb, the archeological team had unleashed an ancient curse that was engraved above the door: 'Death shall come on swift wings to him that touches the tomb of the pharaoh'.

Within two weeks of the tomb's discovery, the main financial backer of the dig, Lord Carnarvon, died. Over the next few years, newspapers reported that a further 26 people involved in the historic find had also passed away. It was rumoured that the curse even affected people when the treasure went on a world tour. Employees at the museums where it was exhibited mysteriously fell ill and died. This was later proved to be purely rumour with no real evidence to support it.

Nowadays few people believe in Tutankhamun's curse. Howard Carter lived to the age of 64, and the artifacts have been on many world tours without anyone being affected by them. Maybe the curse was simply made up by newspaper journalists to sell papers?

THE GREATEST TREASURE YET TO BE FOUND

The tomb of the Qin Shihuang, First Sovereign Emperor of China, is thought to be one of the greatest treasures yet to be uncovered. He became king of the Chinese state of Qin in 246 BC, and is most famous for linking a series of defensive fortresses in the north of the country to create what is now known as the Great Wall of China (see page 97).

Qin Shihuang was a powerful man and was determined to be buried in a style that befitted his status. He ordered the construction of an elaborate tomb and filled it with everything he would need in the afterlife. The tomb was so enormous that it took 700,000 men over 36 years to construct.

The emperor's tomb has long been the stuff of legend. Historians belived that the tomb was destroyed soon after the emperor's death. For over 2,000 years, the only record of its existence were the writings of a Chinese grand historian, Sima Qian, writing 100 years after Qin Shihuang's death.

Sima Qian described a gigantic, underground tomb, which was made to look like the whole of the Chinese Empire. The tomb was lined with bronze and its ceiling studded with jewels. There were seas and rivers flowing with liquid mercury, which were swirled mechanically to keep them moving. Sima Qian said the entire tomb was guarded by legions of model warriors made from a type of clay called terracotta.

In 1974, the first glimpses of this incredible terracotta army were discovered in an underground chamber, dug up by farm workers. Suddenly the existence of the tomb of the First Sovereign Emperor of China seemed possible. Tests on the soil in the mound above the tomb showed high levels of mercury, perhaps leaking from the model's rivers. The site of these mercury finds is thought to actually match the geography of the Chinese Empire, corresponding to areas where the great Yangtze and Yellow rivers would flow.

So if the writings of Sima Qian are true, the tomb holds trees carved from precious green jade, birds and animals in silver and gold, palaces and pavilions, defended by a series of crossbows set to shoot intruders automatically. All this remains undisturbed until archeologists investigating the site can be certain of preserving the treasures within.

THE MOST CONVINCING FORGERIES

THE MOST RIPPING YARN

Jack the Ripper was the name given to a man who murdered a number of women in London's East End, over 120 years ago. The murderer was never caught and no one knows to this day who he was. He was called Jack the Ripper because he cut his victims' throats.

In 1992, a man named Mike Barrett came forward, claiming he had been left a diary by a friend who was now dead. He claimed it was either a diary written by the notorious Jack the Ripper himself or by someone who knew him. The book had remained hidden for 100 years.

In 1993, a book publisher announced that the diary would be published and the world's greatest murder mystery would be solved at last. Over 200,000 people ordered the book. But when the diary was examined by forgery experts it was denounced as a fake. Though it was written in a genuine Victorian scrapbook, the style of the handwriting was too modern. Some pages at the beginning of the scrapbook had been torn out, as if it had originally been written in by someone else. The publishers went ahead and published the diary anyway.

LINCOLN'S LOVE LETTERS

Abraham Lincoln was one of America's most respected and brilliant presidents. He was a master of the English language. In 1929, an article was published in a magazine called *The Atlantic Monthly*, based on letters Lincoln was supposed to have written to a woman. The writing and spelling in the letters was so bad, it is amazing anyone could think Lincoln had really written them. Here is a sample: 'If you git me the dictshinery I can do both speeling and riting better. My hart runs over with hapyness when I think yore name.' In another of the letters he signs his name 'Abe'.

THE OLDEST ANTIQUES FORGERS

By November 2007, George and Olive Greenhalgh from Bolton, England, had been fooling museum experts for over 17 years. From a garden shed, their son Shaun produced fake Egyptian statues, Anglo Saxon jewellery and long lost paintings by famous artists. He also forged letters of authentication in order to convince people that the objects were genuine. George would then go to auction houses and museums with these 'treasures'.

It is estimated that the couple earned over £850,000 from their scam. They paid back over £400,000, but did not go to prison because at 84 and 83, they were considered too old. Their son was jailed for four years.

THE GREATEST ART FORGER

In the 1970s, Tom Keating from London, England, became famous when he admitted having forged paintings in the style of some of the greatest artists that ever lived. His paintings were so authentic that even experts didn't detect them.

Keating's job was restoring paintings. He was a gifted painter, but found it difficult to sell his own paintings or to get accepted by the art world. Keating decided to teach the so-called art experts a lesson. He began painting in the style of famous painters such as Degas, Renoir and Constable. He deliberately left clues in his paintings that showed they were forgeries. He wrote rude remarks which would show up if a painting was examined properly and X-rayed. Experts admit he was so talented that some of his forgeries have never been detected. They suspect he produced 2,000 forged paintings in the style of over 100 different artists.

In 1982, Keating became famous in his own right, with a TV show teaching people how to paint like the great masters.

THE MOST SHROUDED MYSTERY

The Turin Shroud is a strip of linen that some people believe is the cloth Jesus Christ was wrapped in when his body was taken down from the cross and buried. Imprinted on the cloth is the image of a man's face and the shape of his body, showing the terrible signs of a death on the cross.

The shroud, which measures over 4 metres long and about 1 metre wide, has been kept in the cathedral of St John the Baptist in Turin, Italy, since 1578. Experts have carried out extensive tests to discover whether the shroud is genuine or a fake. The results of carbon-dating tests in 1988 dated the cloth to about 1290, but even using modern techniques, it's so far proved impossible to replicate the shroud.

THE DODGIEST DIARIES

In 1983, a German magazine announced that over 50 diaries written by the Nazi dictator, Adolf Hitler, had been found. The magazine said the diaries were written in his handwriting and showed a nicer side to the man who was responsible for the murder of millions of people. Experts studied the diaries, comparing them to other documents written by Hitler, and decided they were genuine. However, they discovered later that the documents they had compared the diaries to were forgeries themselves, produced by a man called Konrad Kujau, who had also written the diaries

THE MOST HILARIOUS HOAXES

THE TACKIEST LIBERTY BELL

The Liberty Bell is one of America's most treasured possessions. It rang for the first time on the 8th of July 1776, to mark the first reading of the Declaration of Independence, which announced that America was now free from British rule. It is an important piece of American history. On the 1st of April 1996, a fast-food chain called Taco Bell announced they had bought the Liberty Bell. They said they were renaming it the Taco Liberty Bell, which horrified the American people.

The situation was made worse when the White House announced that the government would also be selling the Lincoln Memorial, to help reduce the country's debt. The whole country was up in arms. It later turned out that these stories were two of the best April Fools' tricks ever.

THE MOST MUSICAL CARROTS

On the 1st of April 2002, Tesco, a British supermarket, published an advert to say they had special carrots for sale that whistled when they were cooked. The advert said the carrots were grown with air holes, so that you didn't have to test them to see if they were cooked. The carrots told you themselves – by whistling!

THE SILLIEST SPAGHETTI

One of the best April Fools' Day hoaxes took place in 1957. A well-known broadcaster named Richard Dimbleby announced on British television that Switzerland had had a bumper spaghetti crop. The viewers were shown pictures of strands of spaghetti hanging from the branches of trees and people picking them and putting them into baskets. Richard Dimbleby ended the broadcast by saying, 'For those who love this dish, there's nothing nicer than real, home-grown spaghetti.'

Hundreds of people phoned the television station to ask how they could grow their own spaghetti. They were told to, 'place a sprig of spaghetti in a tin of tomato sauce and hope for the best.'

THE MOST TALENTED CHIMPANZEE

In 1964, art critics in Sweden hailed a new star – an exciting French artist with a bold and unique style called Pierre Brassau. His paintings were exhibited in a gallery in Gothenburg, Sweden, and critics praised his work commenting on his 'powerful strokes' and 'clear determination'. One critic said, 'Pierre is an artist who performs with the delicacy of a ballet dancer'. The thing is, Pierre Brassau wasn't a French artist. He wasn't called Pierre, he wasn't a Frenchman – in fact he wasn't a man at all. Pierre Brassau was in fact a four-year-old West African chimpanzee named Peter. Peter lived in Boras Zoo, Sweden. His keeper had been persuaded to give Peter art equipment by a journalist. The journalist was keen to see if art critics would be able to recognise the work as a hoax. Could they tell the difference between the work of a modern artist and a monkey artist?

After eating a lot of paint (apparently his favourite colour was blue), Peter began to put some on the canvas. The journalist chose a few of the best paintings to exhibit. One critic, however, was not fooled by the stunt and complained that the paintings were so bad they could only have been done by a chimp – which just shows, you can't fool everyone.

THE BIGGEST CELEBRATIONS

THE BIGGEST FIREWORKS DISPLAY

One of the most extraordinary firework displays the world has seen was the one that closed the Olympic games in Sydney, Australia, in 2000.

The ceremony began when a rocket extinguished the Olympic flame. Then the Australian Air Force roared overhead at low altitude and ejected their fuel. The fuel was set alight, causing a sheet of flame to spread over the whole of Sydney Harbour. People watching said they could feel the heat. The grand finale was when Olympic rings on the Harbour Bridge turned into a wall of flame and slid gently into the water below. Fireworks were set off all along the Harbour Bridge, from four giant barges and boats in the harbour entrance. The whole thing lasted for 23 minutes and cost approximately £1.5 million.

One of the largest firework displays was in Funchal, Madeira on New Year's Eve 2006. The celebrations involved an ear-splitting 66,326 fireworks that were set off in less than ten minutes.

THE BIGGEST CARNIVAL

The carnival in Rio de Janeiro, Brazil, is the biggest, brashest and noisiest party in the world. It is held every year in early spring, with dancing almost non-stop for four whole days and three nights.

There are thousands of dancers, musicians and performers. The parade of samba dancers consists of 12 samba schools competing against each other. Each school has 5,000 dancers parading in front of up to half a million spectators. The dancers in each group have a unique look, with fantastically elaborate costumes and headdresses in dazzlingly bright colours. Each group dances down a specially-made parade area called the Sambadrome, which is 1 kilometre long.

THE BIGGEST MASKED BALLS

The world's biggest masked balls take place during a carnival in Venice. This carnival is one of the oldest carnivals in the world and was first recorded in 1268. It lasts for two weeks and ends on a day called Shrove Tuesday, also known as Mardi Gras, which means 'Fat Tuesday'.

The Venice Carnival is most famous for its masked balls, which are held all over the city. The costumes and masks people wear are so elaborate they completely disguise the people underneath. When you choose a partner to dance with, you have to try and guess who they are. In the past, wearing masks meant people could behave very differently from how they would normally. Ordinary people and servants dressed up like the rich people, and the nobility dressed up as milkmaids, servants or boatmen.

The masks are made out of papier-mâché, hand-painted and decorated with gold and jewels. Most of the masks cover only half of the face, so that the wearer can talk to people, eat and drink. The masks from the Venice Carnival are so beautiful that people from all over the world collect them.

THE MOST EXPENSIVE WEDDING

The wedding of Vanisha Mittal and Amit Bhatia in 2004 is a strong contender for one of the most expensive weddings. It was estimated to have cost over £28 million. A thousand guests were invited, and each received an invitation that was 20 pages long and bound with real silver. The wedding, held in the romantic city of Paris, France, didn't last just a single day – it included a series of events held over five days. The engagement party was held at the Palace of Versailles with cancan dancers and an enormous fireworks display in the gardens of the Eiffel Tower. Indian film stars and dancers performed at the event and it is thought that Australian popstar Kylie Minogue was paid to perform.

The bride's father was the billionaire Lakshmi Mittal. Mittal is a record-breaker for another reason. In 2004, he bought a 12-bedroom London mansion that has a jewel-encrusted pool. He paid £70 million, which, at the time, made it the world's most expensive house.

A wedding that was, perhaps, more expensive took place in 1981, between the King of Dubai and his bride, Princess Salama. The wedding lasted seven days. The actual ceremony was held in a stadium specially built for the occasion that could hold 20,000 people. It was reported that the all the citizens of Dubai took part in the wedding and were fed by the king. At the time the wedding was estimated to have cost £22 million, but to hold a similar celebration would cost more than three times that today.

THE MOST EXPENSIVE TEA PARTY

Until just over 200 years ago, America was a colony of Great Britain and was ruled by the British Parliament in London. In 1773, an extraordinary event took place which changed the course of American history. This event was known as the Boston Tea Party.

A group of 60 American protesters dressed up as Mohawks (a tribe of Native North Americans) in blankets and feathered headdresses. They climbed on board three British ships that were moored in the harbour in Boston, USA. The men were angry about having to pay a new tax on tea to the British. To show their anger, they dumped 342 chests of tea off the sides of the ships. This tea was valued at £18,000 at the time, which would be over £200,000 in today's money.

The British government was furious. They closed Boston Harbour and put in place harsh laws. This built up more hatred against the British and eventually led to the American War of Independence – which gave America the freedom to govern themselves.

THE FOULEST FASHIONS

THE DAFTEST HAIRSTYLES

In the 17th and 18th centuries, ladies liked 'big' hair and the fashion was for incredibly elaborate hairstyles and wigs. Women's hair was starched and combed over pads made of horsehair or frames until it was very tall. It was then powdered to give it a white finish and decorated. Some ladies added birdcages in which they put real birds, others added miniature castles or tiny ships to recreate famous battles!

These hairstyles took so long to create, that ladies would keep their 'dos' for weeks – without washing them in between. As a result their hair became ideal nests for fleas, head lice and other vermin.

THE MOST TOXIC MAKE-UP

If you see pictures of Queen Elizabeth I of England you will be struck by her flame-red hair and her chalky-white face. If a woman looked like that today, she would probably be considered a bit scary, but in the 1500s it was the height of fashion and women wanted to look just like the queen.

They wore red wigs and powdered their faces. Some went even further to get a ghost-white complexion – they smeared their faces with white lead. White lead is extremely poisonous.

It rotted the women's teeth and turned their skin yellow and green. It ate away the top layer of their skin leaving horrible scars. To cover up the scarring, women put on more lead make-up. Eventually their hair fell out, their eyes swelled up painfully and their lungs were affected. Some women died – making them history's greatest fashion victims.

THE LEAST COMFORTABLE SHOES

Today, high-heeled shoes are as uncomfortable as they are fashionable. Even though experts warn they are bad for the feet and posture, people still wear them, believing they look good. But the pain of high heels is nothing compared to the pain caused by 'foot binding'.

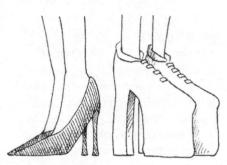

Foot binding was practised in China for over a thousand years, until it was made illegal in 1915. It was fashionable for a woman to have tiny feet, and, if she wanted to marry well, her feet should be no longer than 8 centimetres. In order to achieve this, girls between the ages of three and 11 had their feet soaked in herbs and hot water to soften them. Then all their toes, except their big toes, were broken and folded under the soles of their feet. Eventually their feet were broken across the insteps and bound in a folded position. The pain was excruciating and feet often became infected.

Bound feet were known as 'golden lily feet' because women walked as if they were 'skimming on top of golden lilies'. In fact, the 4.5 billion women believed to have been crippled in this way could hardly walk at all.

THE MOST UNCOMFORTABLE UNDERWEAR

Until well into the 20th century, fashion for women came in all sorts of bizarre shapes and sizes that meant corsets were the only way many women could fit into the most up-to-date outfits.

In Victorian times, it was considered particularly feminine to have a very tiny waist. Women would wear a fabric corset, reinforced with a long narrow piece of wood or steel at the front, and strips of whalebone at the back and sides. The corsets were tightened with laces until their waists were just the right size for their dresses.

Wearing a corset could seriously deform the wearer's ribs, changing the position of her internal organs and limiting her breathing so she was more prone to fainting through lack of oxygen. Even young girls were 'roped in' to this freakish fashion. To prepare them for the proper corsets they would be wearing as adults, young girls would wear training corsets. These garments would shape their figures while they were still growing, so that their lowest ribs would be permanently altered.

THE SEVEN WONDERS OF THE ANCIENT WORLD

A list of the seven most amazing buildings or sculptures in the world was proposed in the 2nd century BC by a writer named Antipater of Sidon. It is limited to the structures that the Ancient Greeks knew about. They are called the Seven Wonders of the Ancient World.

THE GREAT PYRAMID

The Great Pyramid at Giza, Egypt, is both the oldest of the Seven Wonders of the Ancient World and the only one still around today. It was built for King Khufu who died in about 2465 BC, and is said to have taken thousands of men 20 years to construct. According to Herodotus, an Ancient Greek historian, 100,000 men laboured on the pyramid, though archeologists now think the number is more likely to have been about 20,000 men.

The finished pyramid was 147 metres high, which made it the tallest structure made by man for over 4,000 years. It contains 2,300,000 blocks of stone each weighing over 2.25 tonnes. When it was built, the steps were originally capped with pure white limestone that must have shone brilliantly in the desert sun. Sadly, over the centuries the limestone capping was stripped off and now the pyramid is only 138 metres tall.

THE HANGING GARDENS OF BABYLON

Legend has it that King Nebuchadnezzar II, who ruled Babylon, which was located in the south of what is now Iraq, between about 605 BC and 561 BC, built incredible 'hanging' gardens for his wife Amytis. Amytis disliked the dry flat landscape of Babylon, and was homesick for the green hills of Media where she had been born. Nebuchadnezzar made it his mission to recreate these green hills in Babylon.

Nobody is sure exactly where these gardens were or what they looked like. It is thought that they were close to his luxurious palace in Babylon and either consisted of an elaborate roof garden or a series of landscaped terraces. Keeping all these plants watered in the desert was a massive problem, and deep wells, water pumps and a complicated irrigation system were designed specially to keep this miraculous desert garden looking lush.

THE STATUE OF ZEUS

This 12-metre-tall statue of the Ancient Greek god Zeus was located in the Temple of Zeus at Olympia in western Greece. It was built in the 5th century BC, to commemorate the first Olympic Games (see page 129) and was made by a man called Phidias.

Zeus was seated on a throne with his head touching the ceiling of the temple. The statue was covered with solid gold and ivory. In his right hand, Zeus held the figure of Nike, the goddess of victory, and an eagle on a sceptre in his left. The throne was made of cedar wood, decorated with gold and ivory, precious stones and a dark wood called ebony. Some people think the statue was moved to Constantinople, before it was eventually destroyed by fire.

THE TEMPLE OF ARTEMIS

The massive Temple of Artemis was built by King Croesus around 550 BC, in Ephesus, Turkey. It was ransacked and rebuilt a number of times before its eventual destruction. Only fragments of it remain, though archeologists know exactly where it stood.

The temple housed many art treasures and spectacular statues, including one of the goddess Artemis herself, decorated with gold, silver and ebony. The original structure of the temple must have been very impressive, measuring 110 metres by 55 metres. Fragments of the marble columns that held up the roof can be seen in the British Museum, London.

THE MAUSOLEUM OF HALICARNASSUS

This terrific tomb was made to house the body of King Mausolus of Caria, ruler of Persia, who died in 353 BC. It was built by his wife, Artemisia, in Halicarnassus, which is now the city of Bodrum, Turkey. When the queen died two years later, her body was laid to rest there too.

The monument was a huge pyramid with 24 steps, it was 45 metres long and 45 metres tall, with a marble chariot drawn by four horses on the very top. It contained 36 columns. The building was destroyed, most probably by an earthquake, but the word 'mausoleum' is still used today to describe a building used to house a dead body in a tomb.

THE COLOSSUS OF RHODES

The colossus of Rhodes was a giant bronze statue of the Ancient Greek sun god, Helios. It rose an amazing 33 metres and was the tallest statue in the Ancient World. The statue took 12 years to build and stood on Mandráki Harbour on the island of Rhodes, Greece, for only 56 years before it was destroyed by an earthquake in about 226 BC.

THE PHAROS OF ALEXANDRIA

The Pharos of Alexandria was a lighthouse completed in about 280 BC and was used to warn ships of the rocks surrounding the port of Alexandria, Egypt. The building measured over 110 metres to the top. During the day polished bronzed mirrors reflected the sunlight and at night a fire burned that could be seen up to 50 kilometres away. A spiral ramp led from the ground to the top.

This gigantic lighthouse was a real survivor – it stood for over 1,500 years and survived being buffeted by massive waves and countless earthquakes.

It was built by a man called Sostratus who, in order to get the credit for this Wonder of the World, sneakily carved his name into the stone, and plastered over it. On top of the plaster he carved a dedication to the ruler of Egypt. In time, the plaster wore away and his own dedication, 'Sostratus of Cnidos, son of Dexiphanes, to the saviour gods, for sailors', was left permanently displayed.

In 1994, an archeologist located huge masonry blocks believed to be from the lighthouse, which was toppled by an earthquake in the 1300s.

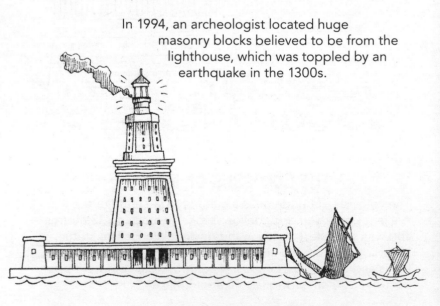

THE NEW SEVEN WONDERS OF THE WORLD

The original Seven Wonders of the World (see pages 92 to 96) may have been considered the best buildings when a Greek scholar drew up the list in the 2nd century BC but the known world was much smaller then than it is today. The list should have been called the Seven Wonders of Southern Europe and North Africa, and it is doubtful that all of the scholars that voted had even seen all of the 'wonders'. On the seventh day of the seventh month, 2007, a new list was announced, voted for by people from all over the world. None of the structures are particularly 'new' but they have an advantage over the first seven – they are all still around today.

THE GREAT WALL OF CHINA

Construction of the Great Wall began during the Qin Dynasty between 221 BC to 206 BC, under the first Sovereign Emperor of China, Qin Shihuang. It was formed from other defensive walls joined together.

The wall is made from stone, rocks, bricks, and packed-earth, and is 4.5 to 9 metres wide and up to 7.5 metres high. It was built by over a million peasants, slaves and prisoners. It was dangerous work, and thousands of these builders died while on the job. Their bodies were added to the rubble inside the wall.

The Great Wall was extensively repaired during the Ming Dynasty of 1368 to 1644, in an attempt to keep out Mongolian invaders. There are approximately 7,300 kilometres of wall in total, although many sections have now disappeared. This makes it the longest construction ever built.

The Great Wall may be vast but, contrary to legend, it cannot be seen by astronauts standing on the surface of the Moon.

CHICHEN ITZA

Most experts agree that the ruined city of Chichen Itza in Mexico was the ceremonial centre of the Maya people from about 550 to 800.

One of the best preserved ruins is a building known as the Temple of Kulkulkan. Kulkulkan was a Maya god and in many carvings he looks like a giant feathered serpent. The temple is a flat-topped, square-based pyramid with 91 steps up each side – one step for each day of the year. The top of the pyramid represents the 365th day. Twice a year, once in the spring and once in the autumn, when the Sun is directly above the equator, shadows are cast on the sides of the pyramid that give the effect of a serpent slithering down the steps.

THE TAJ MAHAL

The Taj Mahal is located in Agra, India. The building was started in 1632, six months after Mumtaz Mahal, the favourite wife of India's then ruler, died while giving birth. Her husband, Shah Jahan, which means King of the World, was broken-hearted by his favourite wife's death and built the Taj Mahal as a memorial to her by the Jumna River, near his palace in Agra. The building is made out of bright white marble and its famous dome stands at 73 metres tall.

PETRA

The beautiful city of Petra, located in Jordan, is made up of buildings carved deeply into desert rock. Experts think that people lived in and around Petra from as early as 1200 BC. During Ancient Greek and Roman times, the city of Petra was one of the most important cities in the area now referred to as the Middle East. People travelled there from all over Europe, Africa and Asia to trade in spices, that were very precious at the time. The city of Petra is literally carved into sandstone cliffs, and its name comes from the Ancient Greek word for rock. The most famous buildings in Petra are the intricately carved tombs that are set into the pinky-orange rock, and some are even used as people's homes.

MACHU PICCHU

Machu Picchu is located high up in the Andes in Peru and was built in the 15th century by an ancient civilisation called the Incas. The Incas started as a small tribe but grew into a great civilisation. At their peak, their empire included most of Peru and stretched south into Argentina and north into Equador.

The Incas were master builders. They had only basic tools and no mortar to fit the giant rocks together, but the stones of their buildings were cut so precisely they fitted together perfectly and still stand today.

THE COLOSSEUM

This ancient amphitheatre is an oval-shaped arena, located in Rome, Italy. It was opened to the public in AD 80, and was designed to hold up to 50,000 cheering and stamping spectators. The upper storey was added in AD 82. Crowds would flock in through any of the 80 entrances to see exotic wild animal shows and watch gladiators fighting to the death.

Despite the damage done by earthquakes and lightning strikes, the Colosseum is still an impressive building and many modern stadiums are modelled on its design. Sadly, over the centuries, the theft of stone has taken chunks out of this ancient arena.

CHRIST THE REDEEMER

This imposing open-armed statue of Jesus Christ measures 38 metres tall and towers over the city of Rio de Janeiro, Brazil. Created in 1931, by a sculptor called Paul Landowski, Christ the Redeemer took five years to build and is the newest of the New Seven Wonders of the World.

THE MOST HAUNTED

THE MOST TERRIFYING TOWER

The Tower of London, found in London, England, is said to be one of the most haunted places in the world. For hundreds of years it was the place where men, women and children, earls, dukes, kings and queens were sent to be imprisoned, tortured and sometimes executed.

One of the most famous ghosts said to haunt the Tower is that of Anne Boleyn. She was the second wife of Henry VIII, King of England. She was beheaded at the Tower in 1536. Her ghost has been seen walking on Tower Green and in a chapel, sometimes carrying her own head. The ghost of King Henry VI is also said to appear on the stroke of midnight on the anniversary of his death. He was held in the Wakefield Tower during the War of the Roses and stabbed to death in 1471.

Another ghost said to haunt the dark corridors of this historic landmark is the White Lady. She has been seen standing and waving at a window, and visitors say they have smelt her perfume as she drifts around St John's Chape

THE CREEPIEST KITCHEN

Over forty years ago, in a house in Bélmez de la Moraleda, Spain, a lady called Maria Gomez claimed she saw a face in the floor of her kitchen. Surprised, she chipped away at the floor to get rid of it and as she did even more faces appeared.

Scientists tried to prove that Maria Gomez must have either been mistaken or that she had painted these faces on the floor herself. The kitchen was closed for three months while they did some tests on the floor, but nothing was discovered and the faces remained. They then dug a trench in the kitchen and discovered bones from a 13th century graveyard. The odd thing was, that although they found the skeletons of bodies buried there long ago, not one of them had a head.

THE MOST PETRIFYING PRISON

The Eastern State Penitentiary in Philadelphia, USA, looks scary enough from the outside. Its dark-stone walls make it look like a massive fortress, with towers and walls nearly 10 metres high.

Charles Dickens, a famous British writer who wrote *A Tale of Two Cities* (see page 124) visited the prison in 1842, and was horrified at the conditions inside. He said that the prisoners were so isolated they must have felt like they had been buried alive. The prisoners were locked alone in their cells all the time, except for two 30-minute exercise periods a day. Some accounts claim that when they were taken out, prisoners had to wear a black hood over their heads so they could not see or talk to anyone. They were so lonely that they would tap messages to each other on the pipes in their cells and try to whisper through the air vents.

Today the building is no longer a prison and is open to the public. Visitors have claimed to be able to hear ghostly whispering and the sound of crying coming from the cells. Some have seen the shape of anguished faces on the walls and distorted forms swirling around.

THE SPOOKIEST PHOTOGRAPH

The most famous ghost photo of all time is the one taken of the Brown Lady walking down the staircase in Raynham Hall, a large country house in Norfolk, England.

The Brown Lady is said to be the ghost of Lady Dorothy Walpole. When her husband, Charles Townshend, found out she had been unfaithful to him, he imprisoned her in the house. He refused to let her leave or even to see her children. She remained imprisoned until the day she died.

Her ghost was seen regularly. When King George IV was staying at the hall he saw a woman in a brown dress standing by his bed. He said she was pale and her hair was untidy.

A photograph of the Brown Lady was taken by two men photographing the house for a magazine in 1936. When they developed one of the pictures they had taken, they saw the image of a ghostly woman walking down the stairs. The picture was later published in a magazine. Since the magazine was published, however, the ghost has hardly ever been seen.

THE BIGGEST AND BEST MUSIC-MAKERS

THE MOST SUCCESSFUL SONGWRITERS

All songs are a combination of two things – the toe-tapping tune and the words. Very often it is the singer of the song that gets the most attention, especially if that person wrote the music, too. This is why you might not have heard of Bernie Taupin, the man who is credited with having written the words to the greatest number of songs, but you will certainly have heard the songs themselves.

Bernie Taupin is most famous for writing the words to the music of Elton John. He wrote many of the songs you will hear in the Disney film *The Lion King* (1994) and also the words to one of the biggest selling singles of all time, *Candle in the Wind*. Bernie and Elton's partnership has lasted more than 40 years. Oddly, most of the songs they wrote were written separately. Bernie would write the words and send them to Elton, who would set them to music. Together, they have produced more than 30 albums, many film soundtracks, several musicals and sold more than 200 million albums.

Madonna is one of the top-selling female recording artists. She has sold over 200 million albums. Her 2009 'Sticky and Sweet' tour was the most successful by a female solo artist, earning more than $408 million.

THE RICHEST MUSICIAN

The world's richest musician isn't Elton John or even Madonna. It is Shake, the lead singer for a band called Manakin. You have probably never heard of him as he didn't make his money from music. Shake is rich, seriously rich, because his personal fortune is thought to come to over a £1 billion. This rocking rich kid is also the official Prince of Pop. Shake, whose real name is Sheikh Hassan bin Rashid Al Khalifa, is a member of Bahrain's royal family.

THE BIGGEST-SELLING SINGLE

It is hard to be precise about, which is the bestselling single of all time, as worldwide sales of records have been calculated only recently, but it is probably one of two songs.

Bing Crosby was a big movie star and singer. It was not surprising that when he sang the song *White Christmas* (1954) in a film of the same title, the track became a big hit. It is thought to have sold over 50 million copies and it is still selling today. Sales of *White Christmas* were only rivalled in 1997, by Elton John and Bernie Taupin's song, *Candle in the Wind*, released to commemorate the death of Princess Diana in that year. Originally written about the actress named Marilyn Monroe, it was rewritten and re-released. The record became an instant smash hit and sold over 37 million copies.

THE MOST SUNG SONGS

HAPPY BIRTHDAY TO YOU

Happy Birthday To You is the most well-known and most-sung song on the planet. It is sung in countries all over the world, and has been translated into many different languages.

Happy Birthday To You may be a worldwide smash hit today, but that isn't how it started out. It wasn't even a song about birthdays. *Happy Birthday To You* was originally *Good Morning To All*. It was a song for nursery-school children to sing at the start of their day, written in 1893, by two teachers, sisters Patty and Mildred Hill, in Kentucky, USA.

The sisters themselves did not earn any money from their creation, and many people think they copied the song from other similar songs around at the time. In 1935, a company 'copyrighted', or registered, *Happy Birthday To You*, with the intention of making people pay to perform the song in public. There has been much disagreement over whether this was legal, but maybe you should think twice next time you are tempted to break into song at a friend's birthday party.

FOR HE (OR SHE) IS A JOLLY GOOD FELLOW

The second most-sung song is usually sung to praise someone or mark an important event in their lives. Nobody is quite sure who wrote the words, but it is thought that it was written in the early 1700s, so it has been around for a long time. The tune was originally taken from a French song, *Malbrouk S'en Va-t-en Guerre*, about a British duke.

Unlike *Happy Birthday To You*, however, you can sing *For He's a Jolly Good Fellow* in public without fearing a fee.

AULD LANG SYNE

This song is sung traditionally on New Year's Eve. It is a nostalgic song about missing home. The words 'auld lang syne' translate approximately as 'days gone by'.

The history of the song is a little unclear. A famous Scottish poet called Robert Burns claimed that he came across a man singing an old folk song and had used the words in his own poem *Auld Lang Syne*, written in 1788. It is true that the *Ballad of Auld Lang Syne* was published in 1711 by a man named James Watson.

SILENT NIGHT

This famous Christmas carol comes from a poem called *Stille Nacht*, written in 1816, by a pastor called Joseph Mohr. The story goes that on Christmas Eve, 1818, Mohr gave his poem to Franz Xaver Gruber, the choir director of a church in Oberndorf, Austria. Within hours, Gruber had written the music to go with it.

The next day was Christmas Day, and the first time that *Silent Night*, the most performed and best-loved Christmas carol of all time, was sung. Some people sing the song with each verse in a different language to remind everyone who hears it that Christmas is being celebrated all over the Christian world.

EXCEPTIONAL INSTRUMENTS

THE LOUDEST MUSICAL INSTRUMENT

The world's loudest instrument is also the world's largest pipe organ. It is the City Convention Hall Organ in Atlantic City, New Jersey, USA. It was built in 1929, and is so large it can take over four hours just to look round it.

The pipe organ is a keyboard instrument a bit like a piano, but instead of the sound being made by hammers hitting strings, the sound is made by air blowing through rows of pipes. The player can control the amount of air in the pipes with 'stop keys' which are pulled out and pushed in, to make the sound loud or quiet.

The City Convention Hall Organ has seven keyboards, 1,439 stop keys and over 33,000 pipes. One of the stop keys produces the loudest musical sound in the world – six times the volume of the loudest train whistle!

Sadly, over the years, many of the organ's moving parts, which are mostly made of leather, have disintegrated. So the organ is now undergoing a restoration programme. Volunteers are working to restore the organ to its former glory, one pipe at a time. It's painstaking work, but they hope that one day the organ will wow a new generation with its amazing sound.

THE LARGEST MUSICAL INSTRUMENT

The Great Stalacpipe Organ, in Virginia, USA, is made of huge stalactites that hang from the roof of the Luray Caves.

Stalactites are formed from dripping water depositing dissolved rock on a cave roof. This dissolved rock solidifies and grows slowly over centuries until it becomes stone and hangs like icicles from the cave roof.

A scientist with the wonderful name of Leland Sprinkle spent three years searching the caves for stalactites which were the right shape and size to produce different musical notes. The ones he chose covered an area of over 14,000 square metres. The stalactites are struck by mallets operated electronically and activated by pressing the keys on a large keyboard. The eerie music can be heard floating throughout the caves without the need of loud speakers

THE SMALLEST MUSICAL INSTRUMENT

An instrument called the nano guitar, which was developed at Cornell University, USA, is the smallest musical instrument in the world. It has six strings and looks very much like a real guitar. However, it is tiny. The length of the guitar is just 10 microns, which makes it about the size of a single red blood cell. Now that's small! Scientists use light from a laser to move the strings of the nano guitar, but as you might imagine, the human ear can't detect the sound it makes.

A musician called G. Jayaprakash has made a tiny musical instrument called a 'sushiri' that you can actually hear. It measures 4.5 centimetres long and 1.5 centimetres wide and weighs half a gram. Made from a chip of wood, you hold it to your lips like a mouth organ and play it with your fingers covering tiny rows of holes.

THE OLDEST MUSICAL INSTRUMENT

In 2012, archeologists found two flutes in a cave in southern Germany. These early instruments, which were made from mammoth tusk and bird bone, have been analysed using carbon-dating. The results show that the flutes were made between 42,000 and 43,000 years ago.

A fragment of hollow bear bone was found in Slovenia in 1995 and dates from as long as 45,000 years ago. But there are doubts over whether it was a flute or the two holes in the bone were made by animals gnawing it.

The oldest known playable instrument was found in central China. The flute is between 7,000 and 9,000 years old and is made from the wing bone of a bird.

THE MOST EXPENSIVE MUSICAL INSTRUMENTS

In March 2008, one of the most expensive instruments ever bought was played in public for the first time in 70 years. It was a violin made in 1741, by one of the world's most famous violin makers, Giuseppe Guarneri. The violin was bought for nearly £2 million at an auction. In July 2010, another Guaneri violin was put up for auction at £11.5 million. Guarneri violins are so expensive because they are very well-made and incredibly rare.

Other famously expensive violins were made by a man called Antonio Stradivari between the years 1698 and 1720. He, and members of his family, are believed to have made 1,100 instruments, of which only about 650 are known to have survived. A single instrument is known as a Stradivarius. In 2011, a Stradivarius was sold at auction for £9.8 million to raise money for victims of the Japan earthquake.

The most famous violin made by Stradivari in the world can be seen, but not heard, at the Ashmolean Museum in Oxford, England. Made in 1716, it has hardly ever been played. It is said Stradivari was so enchanted with the sound he would never sell it. You may never be able to hear the violin, which is called the Messiah violin, as it was given to the museum under the strict condition that it is never played.

FANTASTIC FILMS

THE FIRST PROJECTED PICTURES

The principle of using light to project images onto a wall is ancient. It might even date back to the time when human beings discovered fire, with cave dwellers entertaining each other with hand shadows. There are pictures from the 1500s of people using lamps known as 'magic lanterns' to project pictures onto walls.

Later, people used lanterns to create horrific images of demons and ghosts to frighten audiences. By the 1800s, families were using magic lanterns as a form of home entertainment.

THE FIRST MOVING PICTURES

In 1872, a Californian horse-owner needed to settle a bet – he wanted to know whether a galloping horse lifts all four hooves off the ground at once. He hired a British photographer named Eadweard Muybridge, who set up 48 cameras beside a racecourse. He managed to rig them so they would be triggered as the horse galloped by. The result was one of the first sequences of photographs ever produced. It also settled the bet – a horse does lift all four hooves.

Today, film cameras capture moving images by taking a sequence of individual images of moving objects, known as 'frames'. They take around 24 frames every second. When the pictures are viewed in rapid succession, the human brain perceives the objects shown to be moving, because each image produced in our eyes takes a moment to fade.

In 1894, two brothers named Auguste and Louis Lumière invented a machine called a 'Cinématographe'. It was a box containing a strip of sequential photographs which were projected onto a screen. When viewed, the objects in the images appeared to be moving. These were the first moving pictures. In 1895, the brothers showed ten films using the Cinématographe.

THE OLDEST SURVIVING FILM

The world's oldest surviving celluloid film was made on the 14th of October 1888. It was shot by a French man called Louis Aimé Augustin Le Prince. The film, now called *Roundhay Garden Scene*, shows Le Prince's son, Adolph, and three members of the Hartley family in the garden at Roundhay in Leeds, UK. This film might be the oldest, but don't expect to get through much popcorn as you watch it – the whole film lasts only 2 seconds

THE FIRST FEATURE-LENGTH TALKIE

Did you know that films made before 1927 didn't have any sound? Cinemas would hire pianists or play records during a film to add some drama to what was being shown on screen. The first feature-length 'talkie', a film in which spoken dialogue was used as part of the dramatic action, was called *The Jazz Singer* (1927). It was produced in Hollywood and was a smash hit with audiences.

The Jazz Singer was made using a sound system called 'Vitaphone'. It worked by recording sound on a record as a film was shot. The record was then played while the film was shown.

THE LONGEST FILM

The longest film is a snore-inducing ten *days* long. *Modern Days Forever* (2011) had its one and only screening in Helsinki, Finland. The film was projected onto the side of the Stora Enso building in Helsinki and shows centuries of wear on a building, condensed into ten days. Even so, everyone has to answer a call of nature or ten over the course of ten days viewing, so what would people miss?

When the makers, Superflex, were asked they said, "There is a chance that you might miss a very important point but if you gotta go, you gotta go."

THE MOST OSCARS WON

An Oscar, known as an Academy Award, is the award that most directors and actors hope to win in their careers. The Academy of Motion Picture Arts and Sciences in the USA has put on this prestigious awards ceremony since 1929. Oscars are awarded by the votes of members – and everyone who wins an Oscar becomes a member of the Academy.

Walt Disney won 32 Oscars, more than anyone else. The actor or actress with the most Oscars is Katharine Hepburn, who won four awards for Best Actress. The youngest ever Oscar-winner is an actress called Tatum O'Neal, who was ten when she won Best Supporting Actress for the film *Paper Moon* (1973).

The most Oscars ever won by a single film is 11. Three films have been lucky enough to have achieved this – they are *Ben Hur* (1959), *Titanic* (1997), and *The Lord of the Rings: The Return of the King* (2003). *The Lord of the Rings: The Return of the King* is the only film ever to have won every single Oscar it was nominated for.

THE MOST EXCEPTIONAL OSCAR ACCEPTANCE SPEECHES

Actors receiving Oscars are warned that they have 45 seconds to make an acceptance speech. However, not everyone plays by the rules. The record for the longest acceptance speech is held by Greer Garson. She won the Best Actress Oscar for her role in a film called *Mrs. Miniver* (1942). She started with the words 'I'm completely unprepared' – then she spoke for over five minutes. She never won another Oscar.

One of the funniest comments during a speech was made by Robin Williams, who won an Oscar in 1998 as Best Supporting Actor for his role in *Good Will Hunting* (1997). Williams concluded, 'Most of all, I want to thank my father, up there, the man who when I said I wanted to be an actor, he said, "Wonderful, just have a back-up profession like welding."'

THE BIGGEST MONEY-MAKING MOVIES (US$)

1. *Avatar* (2009)	• made $2,781 million
2. *Titanic* (1997)	• made $1,835.3 million
3. *Harry Potter and the Deathly Hallows: Part 2* (2011)	• made $1,327.6 million
4. *Avengers Assemble* (2012)	• made $1,180.9 million
5. *Transformers: Dark of the Moon* (2011)	• made $1,123.7 million
6. *Lord of the Rings: The Return of the King* (2003)	• made $1,119.9 million
7. *Pirates of the Caribbean: Dead Man's Chest* (2006)	• made $1,065 million
8. *Toy Story 3* (2010)	• made $1,062 million
9. *Pirates of the Caribbean: On Stranger Tides* (2011)	• made $1,041 million
10. *Alice in Wonderland* (2010)	• made $1,023 million

(Source: Worldwide Box Office Sales,
The Internet Movie Database – www.imdb.com)

THE MOST EMBARRASSING MISTAKES ON SCREEN

THE MOST MEDIEVAL MOTORCAR

The film *El Cid* was made in 1961, and nominated for three Oscars, but didn't win any of them. Perhaps this was because the panel noticed a few of the many mistakes that made it onto the screen. *El Cid* is a film about the life of a Spanish king in the 11th century – a time when you would not expect to see a set of tyre tracks in the sand on the beach made by the wheeled camera rig pulling back. Look out for a red car driving through the trees in the background of a goodbye scene.

THE MOST WATCHED WATCH

Titanic (1997) is one of the most expensive and popular films of all time (see opposite) but that doesn't mean it is perfect. In a dramatic scene when the RMS *Titanic*, a huge passenger ship, is sinking and people are getting into lifeboats, one of the passengers can be seen wearing a digital watch. The *Titanic* sank in 1912, long before digital watches had even been invented.

THE MOST MIRACULOUS LAUNDRY

In the following films it would appear that the film-makers of Hollywood have made an amazing new discovery that could make laundry a thing of the past – self-cleaning clothes.

In *Harry Potter and the Philosopher's Stone*, there is a giant dog named Fluffy who drools all over the shirt of a character called Ron Weasley. In the next shot, however, when Ron falls into the Devil's Snare, his shirt is magically clean and dry.

Self-cleaning clothes are not a new invention either. In *The Wizard of Oz* (1939), the main character, Dorothy, falls into a pigpen, but, as if by magic her dress remains completely clean.

THE LEAST ANGELIC ANGELS

You would expect that the three women, known as angels, who feature in a film called *Charlie's Angels* (2000) and devote their lives to fighting crime, would respect the law. However, in the film these hungry heroines see nothing wrong with leaving a restaurant without paying the bill. They go to a drive-through restaurant and order some food. When it is handed to them they drive off without paying. The shame!

THE BEST BOOKS

THE OLDEST BOOK

In 1943, in south-west Bulgaria, workmen digging out a canal uncovered an ancient tomb with paintings on the walls. Inside was what may be the oldest multiple-page book ever found. It has six pages and they are made of pure gold. The book is written in the Etruscan language. The Etruscans were an ancient people who settled in Italy over 3,000 years ago.

There are earlier examples of writing, but these are just single pages. The pages of this book are bound together at one edge, just like a modern book. Inside there are pictures of a horseman, a mermaid and some warriors. The book was donated to Bulgaria's National Museum of History by a man under the condition that his identity was not revealed.

A book that might be the oldest surviving printed book was found early last century, in a sealed cave in north-west China. It is a beautifully illustrated copy of *The Diamond Sutra* – a scroll over 5 metres long, made from seven strips of paper, joined together and printed using carved wooden blocks. It bears the date 868, and is written in Chinese.

THE MOST EXPENSIVE PRINTED BOOK

When it was sold for over £7.3 million in 2010, a copy of John James Audubon's *Birds of America* became the most expensive book ever sold. Audubon was born in France. At the age of 18 he was sent to America to escape being forced to join the army. He was a brilliant wildlife illustrator, and studied and drew every species of bird found in North America. *Birds of America* is a big book, measuring 102 centimetres in height and 74 centimetres wide. It was the first book to show life-size birds in their natural surroundings. Every page shows a detailed hand-coloured engraving of a different species. There are 435 prints in total and only 120 copies of the book are known to exist today.

THE MOST EXPENSIVE COMIC BOOK

The world's most valuable comic book is *Action Comics No.1* from 1938. Written by Jerry Siegel and illustrated by Joe Shuster, this comic gave us our first superhero ... is it a bird, is it a plane ... it's Superman! In 2011, a copy of *Action Comics No.1* was sold for £1.4 million. The cover price was ten cents.

THE LONGEST BOOK

Yongle was an emperor who ruled China between 1402 and 1424. The Emperor ordered an encyclopedia to be compiled by a scholar called Xie Jin. However, the book wasn't long enough for the emperor's liking and he ordered that more people be brought in to work on the project. So, for four years, thousands of scholars researched and wrote entries.

The encyclopedia was finally completed in 1408. It contained 22,937 chapters that were bound into 11,095 volumes. The Chinese language is written using characters to represent whole words or ideas – this book has 370 million characters.

Even today, the *Yongle Dadian* would still win the title of the longest book. Sadly, fewer than 400 of the original volumes still exist. Some historians believe they were buried with Emperor Jiajing (1521–66) in his tomb.

THE BESTSELLING BOOKS OF ALL TIME

THE CHRISTIAN BIBLE

(estimated sales of up to 6 billion)

The Bible wasn't originally written as one book. It is a collection of stories and accounts by lots of different authors written over a thousand years. The first part of The Bible, known as The Old Testament, was written in Hebrew and covers the years 1000 BC to 100 BC. The other part, The New Testament, about the life of Jesus Christ and the early Christian Church, was written in Ancient Greek during the 1st century AD. It has since been translated into almost every language.

There is an organisation called Gideon's International that is dedicated to distributing Bibles and is most famous for putting free Bibles in hotel rooms throughout the world.

QUOTATIONS FROM THE WORKS OF MAO ZEDONG

(estimated sales of between 900 million and 6 billion)

Quotations from the Works of Mao Zedong was produced in 1966, by the then Chinese leader, Mao. It was law for everyone in China to carry a copy with them at all times or risk punishment. It might be fair to say that this bestselling book was not necessarily the most popular book, or even the most read book – just the book most carried-about!

If the sales figure of 6 billion copies of *Quotations from the Works* of Mao Zedong is true, this would mean that there was one book printed for almost every single person living on the planet, or at least four-and-a-half copies each for every person living in China.

THE CHINESE DICTIONARY – XINHUA ZIDIAN

(estimated sales of up to 400 million)

It is estimated that one in three Chinese-speakers owns a copy of this book, and there are over 1.3 billion people living in China alone. First published in 1953, it was the work of many scholars working over a period of hundreds of years. Written Chinese uses 'characters' to show whole words in simplified pictures. For example, the character for 'field' is a square divided into four. Each Chinese character is made up of around two to four basic characters called 'radicals'. Extra strokes are added to show how the word should be said.

THE QUR'AN

(estimated sales of 200 million)

The Qur'an is the sacred book of Islam. It was written down between 610 and 632 in classical Arabic. It contains all the guidance necessary for Muslims in their lives. It has been translated into other languages, but it is thought by some to be untranslatable.

'A TALE OF TWO CITIES' BY CHARLES DICKENS
(estimated sales of 200 million)

The first work of fiction in this bestseller list is *A Tale of Two Cities*. It hit the shelves in 1859, but not all in one go. Today the novel can be bought in one book, but Charles Dickens wrote this book in weekly instalments in a magazine called *'All Year Round'*. Readers had to wait for the next edition to find out what happened next. When the first part of the work was published the last part hadn't even been written, and it is not known whether even Dickens knew how the story would end.

'LORD OF THE RINGS' BY J.R.R TOLKIEN
(estimated sales of 150 million)

J.R.R Tolkien's publisher had been so pleased by the success of his book, *The Hobbit*, written 17 years earlier, that they asked for a sequel. *The Lord of the Rings* was divided into three volumes that were published one after another between 1954 and 1955. This was done to limit the risk of publishing such a large book. The publisher was concerned it would lose money. They needn't have worried – *The Lord of the Rings* has been popular since the day the first book was published. The story has now been made into a blockbuster series of three films (see page 116).

RECORD-BREAKING WRITERS

THE MOST PROLIFIC WRITER

British author Dame Barbara Cartland published an incredible 723 books in her career, making her the most prolific author of the 20th century. Most of her books were romantic novels. Cartland didn't actually write these books, instead she told the stories aloud to her secretaries, who typed them as she spoke. She employed up to six secretaries at a time to cope with all the work. Up until 1977, she managed to write an amazing ten books a year, but as demand for her books grew, she managed to increase that to 20 books a year. That is as much as one full novel every 18 days. She continued to write novels at that rate for the next 20 years.

When Cartland died aged 99 in May 2000, 160 unpublished manuscripts were found in her home. In total her books have sold over a billion copies and have been translated into 38 different languages.

THE MOST POPULAR LIVING WRITER

J.K Rowling's books about a young wizard named Harry Potter have sold over 450 million copies around the world. That figure gets bigger every day. Although the books were written for children, like all great children's stories, they are read by people of all ages around the world.

The books, of which there are seven in the series, are available in 200 countries and have been published in over 75 languages, including Latin!

Not only are the books a publishing phenomenon, but the Harry Potter films based on the books have become one of the most successful series of films ever (see pages 116 and 118). The success of the books and the films has made Rowling one of the richest people in the United Kingdom and the first author to make a billion dollars.

THE ART OF THE BEST

THE OLDEST WORKS OF ART

The oldest known paintings in the world were discovered as recently as 1994, at Vallon-Pont-d'Arc in southern France. About 300 superb paintings and at least that many engravings dating back over 31,000 years were found in the Chauvet cave. Many animals from the Iron Age are depicted – mammoths, rhinos, bears – as well as three animals never seen in cave paintings before – an owl, a panther and a hyena.

THE FIVE MOST EXPENSIVE PAINTINGS

The paintings below are some of the most expensive sold at auction, with prices adjusted for inflation. Many paintings in museums would fetch more but are unlikely to be sold.

1. $119.9 million. *The Scream* by Edvard Munch. Sold 2012.
2. $111.7 million. *Nude, Green Leaves and Bust* by Pablo Picasso. Sold 2010.
3. $109.5 million. *Garcon à la pipe* by Pablo Picasso. Sold 2004.
4. $106.4 million. *Dora Maar au Chat* by Pablo Picasso. Sold 2006.
5. $98.2 million. *Portrait of Adele Bloch-Bauer II* by Gustav Klimt. Sold 2006.

THE MOST UNAPPRECIATED ARTIST

Today, Vincent van Gogh is one of the most valued artists of all time. In recent years, his paintings have sold for record-breaking sums of money. However, he only managed to sell one painting before he died in 1890, at the age of 37.

THE BEST BARGAIN HUNTER

A retired American lorry driver called Teri Horton may have found the best bargain of all time when she purchased a painting for £2.50 from a second-hand shop in the early 1990s. Horton claims she bought it to cheer up a friend. Unfortunately, the painting was too big for her friend's home, so Horton put it in a garage sale. A local art teacher spotted it and decided it might be a painting by a famous artist called Jackson Pollock.

Since then, Horton has struggled to have the painting declared a genuine Pollock. So far she has been unsuccessful, despite claims that the artist's fingerprint has been found in the paint on the canvas. Her story has since been made into a documentary and Horton has appeared on television shows all across America. She says she will burn the painting rather than sell it for under £25 million. Seeing as one of Jackson Pollock's paintings sold for almost £70 million, this would make Horton's painting a bit of a bargain.

THE LARGEST NUMBER OF
MISSING PAINTINGS

On the 7th of July 2010, a painting of the city of Rome, Italy, sold at auction for a whopping £29.72 million and became one of the most expensive paintings by an English artist ever sold. This painting was by an artist named J.M.W. Turner. Today, Turner is probably Britain's most famous painter, but this wasn't always the case.

During his lifetime, Turner's style was not popular, but after his death, people began to look at his work differently. They realised that his paintings were actually brilliant, but by then it was too late, as many of his paintings could not be found. They had not been stolen; they had just disappeared, having been hidden away in cupboards and attics because people didn't like them and forgot about them.

In 2002, the Tate Gallery in London began a search. Drawings and engravings of all Turner's missing paintings along with any information that the gallery had about them were put on a website. As a result, many of Turner's paintings started turning up all over the place, having been forgotten and neglected for years. Nobody realised they were Turners, or even that they were important. So far over 500 missing masterpieces have been found.

THE GREATEST SPORTING EVENTS

THE FIRST OLYMPIC GAMES

The ancient Greeks believed that the hero Hercules founded the Olympic Games in honour of his father, Zeus, the king of the gods. The first recorded Games were held in 776 BC, and a naked runner named Coroebus, who was a cook, won the only event. The event was called the 'stade' and it was a run of about 192 metres. The word 'stadium' comes from 'stade' and is the name given to the type of building where many of the Olympic events are held today. Other events, such as wrestling and chariot races, were added later.

The Games continued to be held every four years until around AD 400, when the Roman Emperor Theodosius I, abolished them. They weren't held again until nearly 1,500 years later.

In 1896, the first modern Olympic Games opened in Athens, Greece. It included many events, such as the pole vault, sprinting, shot-put, weight-lifting, cycling, target-shooting, tennis, a marathon, and gymnastics. Swimming events also took place, but not in vast pools – the swimmers swam in the Bay of Zea, in the Mediterranean Sea. Alfred Hajós, who won gold medals in two of the swimming events, complained of the cold water and towering waves, saying that during the swim, 'My will to live totally overcame my desire to win.'

THE FIRST MARATHON

Training for a modern marathon requires a lot of dedication and hard work. Elite athletes train for months to make sure they are in peak physical condition. They go on special diets, eating food that is very high in energy in the days before the event, all in an attempt to get them through the gruelling race. The first marathon runner in history was not so lucky.

In 490 BC, the Athenian army won a battle over the Persians at the Battle of Marathon. According to legend, the jubilant Athenians decided to send a messenger from Marathon to Athens to announce their victory. The Greeks sent their best runner, Pheiddippides (fi-DIP-i-dees). He had already run 240 kilometres in 2 days to get help from the Spartans, then, after a full day's fighting, he managed to cover the distance of just over 40 kilometres in only 3 hours. It is said that soon after delivering news of the Athenian victory, Pheiddippides dropped dead from exhaustion. This heroic run may have been his last, but it was the first ever marathon.

Centuries later, in 1896, the marathon was run again when the Greeks introduced the event into their Olympic Games. Inspired by the legendary messenger's route, the race was run from Marathon to the Olympic Stadium in Athens. A Greek man named Spiridon Louis won the race in just 2 hours, 58 minutes, 50 seconds.

Today, the marathon that runners complete is 42.195 kilometres long. The distance was changed in 1908, so that the race could cover the distance between Windsor Castle and the White City Stadium in London, England. The extra 2 kilometres were added so that the race would end directly in front of King Edward VII's royal box.

The North Pole Marathon is by far the coldest marathon on Earth and is also the race run furthest north. The runners must cover a distance of just over 42 kilometres on snow-covered ice that is more than 2 metres thick, in the frozen Arctic Ocean.

The race takes place in April and starts very early in the morning. The runners run in temperatures that are well below freezing and can even be as low as −30°C. In 2008, Byeung Sik Ahn finished the race in just over 4 hours, 2 minutes and 37 seconds.

THE LONGEST, HOTTEST RUN

In 2006, three runners, Charlie Engle, Kevin Lin and Ray Zahab, completed a run that could claim the title of the longest and hottest. They ran up to 97 kilometres every day for a total of 111 days. If that wasn't enough, they ran this distance across the world's largest desert, the Sahara (see page 215) where temperatures reached over 52°C. They started in Senegal and finished in Cairo, Egypt. They ran through six countries and travelled 6,920 kilometres. A film named Running the Sahara (2008) was made about their incredible journey.

THE LONGEST TENNIS MATCH

The longest tennis match ever recorded was played in June 2010, during the first round of the Wimbledon tournament in London. American John Isner and Frenchman Nicolas Mahut fought a match that lasted 11 hours and 5 minutes. Play stretched over three days and the players went through 40 bottles of water and seven rackets. The final score was: 6–4, 3–6, 6–7, 7–6, 70–68.

After reaching tie-breaks in sets three and four, the very well-matched players reached a deadlock in the fifth set, which can't be decided by a tie-break. Isner eventually triumphed, but was completely exhausted, and two days later lost his next match 0–6, 3–6, 2–6 in just 74 minutes.

THE WEIRDEST
SPORTING EVENTS

THE MOST RIDICULOUS REGATTA

If you visit the town of Dinant, Belgium, on an August afternoon, you might see the International Regatta of the Bathtubs, at which a fleet of decorated bathtubs are rowed, paddled and pushed down the River Meuse. The rules are simple – no bathtub can be fitted with a motor, and competitors must not try to sink each other. Throwing buckets of water at other competitors and spectators, however, is allowed.

There are prizes for the tub that reaches the finish line the fastest and prizes for the most creative of crafts. Since the event began in 1982, there have been bathtubs carrying butchers with meat knives, a tub full of pirates and even cyclists pedalling their bathtub!

THE MUDDIEST EVENT

Bog Snorkelling takes place in August on Bank Holiday Monday in a thick bog next to a town that claims to be the smallest town in Britain – Llanwrtyd Wells in Wales. A 55-metre-long trench is cut through a muddy bog and competitors must make their way through the cold, muddy water in the quickest time possible. No swimming strokes are allowed – competitors can only use flipper power to wriggle their way through the murky depths. People come from all over the world, armed with snorkels, flippers and wet suits, to take part.

In 2006, the race ended with a tie – both Haydn Pitchforth and Glenn Marshall doggy-paddled to the finish line in exactly 1 minute and 42 seconds. In a rematch, called a 'bog-off', Haydn beat Glenn by one second. In 2011 the record for the fastest time was broken by Andrew Holmes, who finished in 1 minute 24 seconds.

THE LONGEST PANCAKE RACE

Pancake Day is celebrated on Shrove Tuesday, which is the day before the beginning of a period called 'Lent' in the Christian calendar. Traditionally, pancakes were eaten on this day so people could clear their cupboards of ingredients that they weren't allowed to eat during Lent.

The first pancake race took place in 1445, in Olney in Buckinghamshire, England – but it wasn't much of a race. One story claims that only a single runner took part. A woman cooking pancakes heard the church bell chiming and, thinking she would be late for church, ran all the way there still holding her frying pan with a pancake in it.

Since then, there has always been a pancake race in Olney. It starts with the church bell ringing and the contestants run between the Market Square and the church, a distance of about 380 metres, tossing their pancakes as they run. The fastest time was by Devon Byrne who ran the distance in 58.5 seconds in 2012.

There is also a pancake race every year in a town called Liberal, in Kansas in the USA.

THE BIGGEST FOOD FIGHT

In the small town of Buñol, Spain, a festival called 'La Tomatina' takes place every year on the last Wednesday in August. The festival is said to have begun in 1944 as a simple tomato fight between a group of friends, and has now become what some people call the world's biggest food fight.

Every year, over 20,000 people travel to the town to join in the fun. Shops and houses in the main square, the Plaza del Pueblo, cover their fronts with plastic sheeting and La Tomatina begins. Over the next few hours, people throw 125,000 kilograms of ripe or rotten tomatoes at each other. There is only one rule – tomatoes must be squashed in the hand before they are thrown. Afterwards, people wash themselves in the showers that have been specially put up, and the square is cleaned.

THE CHEESIEST EVENT

For 200 years, the Coopers Hill Cheese Rolling and Wake has been held on Coopers Hill near Brockworth in Gloucestershire, England. The event was originally just for the local villagers, but now people come from all over the world to take part.

A large, circular Gloucester cheese is rolled down the hill and the competitors race after it. The first person over the finishing line at the bottom of the hill wins the cheese. The hill is extremely steep, so competitors do their best to keep up, half rolling, half tumbling to the bottom. There are usually plenty of cuts and bruises and even some broken bones at the end of the race. In 2010, the official race was cancelled due to the huge crowds it attracts. In 2011, an unofficial event was organised, in order to keep the tradition alive.

THE BIGGEST SPORTING ARENAS

THE BIGGEST SPORTS STADIUM

The Rungnado May Day Stadium in North Korea is the biggest sports stadium in the world. It was opened on the 1st of May 1989, and has seats for 150,000 people. Its roof is made up of 16 arches arranged in a circle and is said to look like a giant magnolia flower or a parachute.

The largest crowd to fit into the stadium was 190,000 on the 29th of April 1995, when spectators flocked to see a bout of professional wrestling. As well as sporting events, the stadium is also used to stage massive parades and acrobatic displays.

THE BIGGEST SWIMMING POOL

The biggest swimming pool in the world is the San Alfonso del Mar in the holiday resort of Algarrobo, Chile. The giant pool was completed in December 2006. It is just over a kilometre long and has an area of 80,000 square metres – which is just bigger than 11 full-sized football pitches. The pool is filled with 250 million litres of salt water that is pumped in from the Pacific Ocean, and is enjoyed by people sailing small boats as well as bathers.

THE DEEPEST INDOOR SWIMMING POOL

Most recreational pools you will swim in have a shallow end and a deep end, but none has a deep end quite like the pool at Nemo 33, a recreational diving centre in Brussels, Belgium. Built in 2004, the pool is filled with 2.5 million litres of spring water. Visitors can watch divers in the pool through underwater windows. There are flat platforms at different depths and even artificial caves to explore, but the central pit goes down to a depth of 33 metres – there is no shallow end.

THE HIGHEST DIVING BOARD

Most high-diving boards are built at around 24 metres high, which is thought to be the highest height from which it is safe for an experienced diver to dive without serious injury.

Some people make the dangerous sport of high diving look easy. World champion Dana Kunze holds the record for the highest dive, managing to do a reverse triple somersault from a board into a pool 52 metres below.

The highest dive ever attempted was from 60 metres, but, tragically, the diver broke his spine in the attempt.

THE BIGGEST ICE RINK

Mexico City is one of the largest cities in the world and has a population of around 20 million. With an average temperature of around 20°C it is not perhaps the first place you would think there would be an open-air ice rink – but there is, and it is massive. When this gigantic 3,150 square metre rink opened on the 2nd of December 2007, it was the biggest in the world. It can be found in the heart of Mexico City. Apart from its enormous size, the best thing about this rink is that there is no charge to use it and visitors can borrow skates for free.

THE LONGEST SKI SLOPE

The snowy peaks of Mount St Elias in Alaska rise to 5,489 metres high, and then drop straight down to sea level on steep slopes of about 60 degrees. In 2007, two Austrian skiers, Axel Naglich and Peter Ressmann, were the first to successfully ski the 20 kilometres from the top of the mountain down to the sea. It took them 11 days to climb the mountain and three days to ski down. The descent, with its steep ice-covered slopes, deep, narrow valleys and glaciers, could easily have cost them their lives.

THE HIGHEST PRIZE MONEY

THE HIGHEST PRIZE MONEY IN GOLF

How does the chance of winning £5 million sound? Good? Well you had better start practising your putting. In 2007, a new golf tournament called the FedEx Cup was launched, which pitted the world's greatest golfers against one another. They played three tournaments, during which the 144 players who started the competition were whittled down to just 30 who then took part in the final. The gruelling process was certainly worth the bother though, as the winner pocketed £5 million.

Tiger Woods, from the USA, is the player who has earned the most prize money in his career. In 2009, he became the first sports star to earn $1 billion.

There is a legend that claims golf started among a group of shepherds looking after their sheep near St Andrews, Scotland. To pass the time, they competed against each other, hitting stones into rabbit holes with their wooden crooks. Whatever its history, golf has been played for over 500 years.

THE HIGHEST PRIZE MONEY IN TENNIS

The highest prize money in tennis is offered at the Wimbledon Championships, held in London. In 2012, the men's and women's winners each received £1.15 million. The total prize money for all the players involved came to £16.06 million. 2007 was the first year that the women tennis players were able to compete for the chance of winning the same prize money as the men.

Wimbledon is the oldest major tennis championship. It began in 1877 with one event, the Gentlemen's Singles, which was won by Spencer Gore. Around 200 spectators paid a shilling, which is about 5 pence in today's money, to watch the match.

THE BIGGEST LOTTERY WIN

One prize that is available to even the least sporty competitor is a lottery jackpot. On 30th March 2012, the biggest jackpot was the Mega Millions in the United States. Three winners shared a jackpot totalling $656 million. Now that's lucky!

But money doesn't always bring happiness. On Christmas Day, 2002, Andrew Whittaker from the United States became a very rich man. He had won the Powerball Lottery jackpot totalling £158.4 million. At the time it was the biggest lottery prize ever won by a single person.

Mr Whittaker was a religious man and wanted to give some of his winnings to other people. He paid for two churches to be built and set up a fund for people who weren't as lucky as he had been. But Mr Whittaker was inundated with thousands of begging letters from people asking him for money to buy everything from houses and cars to carpets. He gave away over £25 million of his winnings. Things got even worse when his home and business were broken into over and over again. Mr Whittaker is reported to have regretted buying the winning ticket so much that he even said, 'I wish I'd torn up the darn ticket,' because of all the trouble it had brought him.

THE MOST AMUSING AMUSEMENT PARKS

THE OLDEST AMUSEMENT PARK

In 1583, a woman called Kirsten Pill discovered a spring of pure water in Dyrehaven Park near Copenhagen, Denmark. The water from this spring was thought to be able to heal sick people. People from all over Denmark came to visit the spring and they were followed by jugglers and acrobats and magicians, all wanting to make money by entertaining them. Over time, people began to visit more for the entertainments and now the spring is the site of the Bakken Amusement Park.

Today, Bakken claims to be the world's oldest amusement park. It entertains visitors with rides, restaurants and roller coasters. One of their roller coasters, a wooden coaster opened in 1932, is one of the oldest in the world. In August each year, clowns from all over the world come to Bakken to celebrate an international clown festival.

THE TALLEST, FASTEST ROLLER COASTERS

When it opened in 2005, Kingda Ka at the Six Flags Great Adventure (a theme park in New Jersey, USA) became the tallest and fastest roller coaster on the planet. The coaster climbs a tower, twisting at an angle of 90 degrees until it reaches a height of 139 metres and then comes spiralling down.

It is no longer the fastest, though. The Formula Rossa coaster, unveiled at Ferrari World in Abu Dhabi in 2010, accelerates to a truly terrifying 240 kilometres per hour!

THE FIRST FERRIS WHEEL

The Ferris wheel was invented by George W. Ferris, a bridge builder in Pennsylvania, USA, for the World's Fair held in Chicago in 1893. The wheel was 251 metres around the rim, and 80 metres high. It had 36 wooden cars that each held 60 people. Although it was taken down in 1904, the idea survived and has since been copied all over the world.

THE BIGGEST FERRIS WHEEL

Several countries have plans for giant Ferris wheels, which will dwarf the tallest Ferris wheel in the world, the Singapore Flyer, which stands at only 165 metres tall. Projects have been outlined for wheels in Beijing and Moscow, but they are yet to begin. In Las Vegas, United States, work has begun on two Ferris wheels. One, the Las Vegas High Roller, will be 167.6 metres tall, so it will claim the record if it is completed.

THE BIGGEST MAZE

The largest permanent maze in the world is Samsø Labyrinten, on the Danish island of Samsø. It covers 60,000 square metres and its paths total more than 5 kilometres. Tall trees form the walls of the maze, many wild animals and flowers live there, and the paths are decorated with carved wooden statues.

Another of the largest permanent mazes in the world is the 11,215 square metre Peace Maze in County Down, Northern Ireland, opened in 2001 to celebrate peace in the country after many years of conflict between the Protestants and Catholics who live there.

THE BEST TOYS

THE BIGGEST HULA HOOP

The 'Hula' is actually a dance, which comes from Hawaii. To dance the Hula, you need to swivel your hips in a similar motion needed to keep up a hula hoop.

In September 2010, a man called Ashrita Furman spun a hula hoop three and three quarter times around his body. Normally, that would not get into any record books, but Ashrita's hula hoop measured 5.04 metres across.

THE MOST EXPENSIVE TOY CAR

A model of the Bugatti Veyron, made from 24-carat gold, platinum and diamonds is pricey enough at a cool £2 million – roughly the price of two real Veyrons. But it looks like this record is set to be smashed by a scale model of a Lamborghini Aventador LP 700-4. Dripping with diamonds from the seat to the steering wheel, it has been valued at £2.9 million, ten times the cost of the real car!

THE BIGGEST YO-YO

Big Yo is one of the world's largest wooden yo-yo, with a diameter of 80 centimetres. It was first yo-yoed from a crane in San Francisco in October 1979.

Students at Bay de Noc Community College, Escanaba, United States, recently built the largest working yo-yo, with a diameter of 3.51 metres. It was dropped from a height of over 30.4 metres.

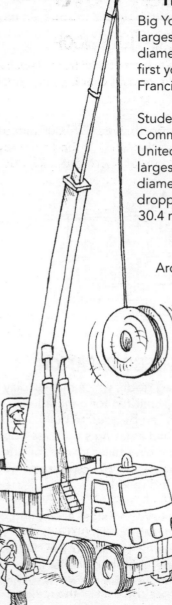

THE OLDEST TOY

Archeologists excavating a site on the island of Pantelleria, Italy, discovered the remains of a 4,000-year-old doll, which may be the world's oldest toy.

It was found in the remains of a hut in what was a Bronze Age village, with miniature pots and plates – possibly part of an ancient toy kitchen. The doll's stone head is 3 centimetres long and carved with eyes, nose and mouth and wavy hair. Some people call it the 'Barbie of the Bronze Age'.

THE MOST EXPENSIVE DOLLS' HOUSE

One of the most expensive dolls' house is worth even more than some people's real homes. It measures just over 2 metres by 1.5 metres and is a replica of Spencer House, a real palace in London. This plush play-palace was built by a company that specialises in making dolls' houses in Bath, England, for a customer from the USA.

The house is estimated to be worth over £200,000, and the carpets alone cost £3,000 to make.

THE LARGEST LEGO CREATION

The word 'lego' is short for 'leg godt', which means 'play well' in Danish. Lego® has amused children for generations. The iconic, colourful plastic bricks can be used to build almost anything. The challenge to build amazing structures from it has resulted in people creating ever taller towers, bridges people can walk across and even, in 2009, a full-scale house complete with working taps and toilet!

The house was built at Denbies Wine Estate in Dorking, Surrey by a man named James May and a team of over 1,200 volunteers, who used more than 2.4 million bricks. Sadly, the house was demolished, as a permanent place for it couldn't be found. May, who slept in the house before it was knocked down, said, 'The bed was a bit hard'.

LIVING MARVELS

ANIMAL RECORD-BREAKERS

THE STRONGEST CREATURE

The horned dung beetle, small enough to sit in the palm of your hand, is the world's strongest creature. This beetle can carry things that are 1,141 times its own weight. That's the equivalent of a human pulling six fully-loaded double-decker buses! It's not the only beetle with brute-strength. The little rhinoceros beetle is also amazingly strong. It can carry things 850 times its own weight.

THE BIGGEST LAND MAMMAL

The African elephant can grow to over 3 metres tall and can weigh as much as 6,350 kilograms, which is as heavy as 90 people. According to San Diego Zoo, the largest-ever elephant weighed 10,886 kilograms and was 3.96 metres tall at the shoulder. It gets to this size just by eating leaves and grass so, if you want to grow up big and tall, make sure you eat your greens!

Despite its enormous size, an elephant can move very quietly – its flat feet are like giant cushions.

THE BIGGEST MAMMAL

Blue whales are the largest animals on Earth. They can grow 30 metres long and weigh up to a massive 180 tonnes. An adult blue whale's heart is about the same size as a small car. The blood vessel which carries blood to the heart is big enough for a person to crawl through.

The blue whale also wins the title of the loudest mammal on Earth. Its calls can be heard many kilometres away. The noise level has been estimated to be around 188 decibels – that's louder than a jet plane. The whale's calls are so low that they are out of human hearing range and specialized equipment is needed to record the rumbling sound.

THE SMALLEST MAMMAL

The bumblebee bat, also known as the Kitti's hog-nosed bat, is between 29 and 34 millimetres long. It lives in West Thailand and nests in warm limestone caves. It has large ears and a snout like a pig. The bumblebee bat weighs just two grams, which is less than a one-pence piece.

THE TALLEST MAMMAL

An adult giraffe can be as tall as 5.5 metres, which is high enough to look into the window on the second storey of an average building. Giraffe calves are 1.8 metres tall when they are born and grow so fast that they can double in height in their first year. Unsurprisingly, giraffe babies don't play very much as they need their energy for growing.

A giraffe's neck can be as long as 1.8 metres, but has exactly the same number of bones as a human neck – seven (they are just a lot longer). They rest their necks over their backs while they are asleep, although adult giraffes don't sleep very much.

The long neck causes some problems. To bring its head down to drink, a giraffe has to open its front legs very wide to be able to reach the water. In this awkward position, it is an easy target for predators.

THE FIVE HEAVIEST LAND MAMMALS

Elephant	Up to 6,350 kilograms
Hippopotamus	Up to 3,628 kilograms
Rhinoceros	Up to 2,267 kilograms
Giraffe	Up to 1,905 kilograms
Water buffalo	Up to 1,179 kilograms

THE BIGGEST SPIDER

The bird-eating goliath tarantula lives on the jungle floors of South America. One of the largest specimens that's been found had a leg-span of 28 centimetres – that's enough to cover a dinner plate. Its fangs and a large hairy body make it look scary, but its bite isn't that dangerous.

It does not build webs to trap prey, but instead pounces on birds, insects and other small mammals.

THE BIGGEST SNAKE

The reticulated python holds the world record for being the longest snake. One found in Indonesia in 1912 measured 10 metres in length. Like other boa constrictors, the reticulated python kills by wrapping itself around its prey, crushing it to death. It then swallows its prey whole.

The reticulated python may be longer, but the title 'King of Snakes' must go to the anaconda. This South American boa constrictor can have a similar girth to that of a man and is able to swallow whole deer and even take on crocodiles.

Despite its ferocious man-eating reputation, the anaconda is actually quite a shy animal that prefers to live by itself by rivers and lakes, slipping into the water when disturbed rather than attacking.

THE LONGEST WORM

The bootlace, or ribbon worm, from Europe, gets its name because that is what it looks like. It grows to between 2.5 centimetres and 30 metres long, and it can stretch much longer. It is not only the world's longest worm, it is the longest living animal.

These worms are greedy meat-eaters. They eat live prey, or carrion – animals that are already dead – by shooting out a long thin proboscis, or sucking tube. The worm then pulls its prey towards its hungry mouth.

THE LONGEST SQUID

The colossal squid is a mysterious monster of the deep with long tentacles covered in hooks and a sharp beak. Until recently only smaller ones had been caught and evidence of bigger squids only came from the stomachs of sperm whales that had eaten them. In 2007 the largest ever squid was caught in Antarctica and measured nearly 12 metres long. It is thought that the colossal squid could grow to 15 metres – longer than two double-decker buses put together and even longer than the giant squid.

THE FASTEST BIRD

Skydiver and film-maker, Leo Dickinson, dived off a 914-metre-high cliff in the Italian Alps at the same moment as a peregrine falcon. He calculated that the speed the falcon reached as it swooped down the cliff face was over 321 kilometres per hour.

THE SLOWEST MAMMAL

Across the ground, a sloth moves at a top speed of 1.5 metres per minute. A sloth spends most of its time hanging upside down from the branches of trees on its hook-like toes. When it moves in the trees it swings gently from branch to branch at a sedate 3 metres per minute. It is so slow that algae can grow in its fur, making it appear green and blend into its jungle background. The sloth sleeps hanging upside down and because of this its fur grows in the opposite direction to that of other animals. This is so that when it rains, the water runs off.

THE FASTEST MAMMAL

If a cheetah was running on a motorway, it would definitely have to be in the fast lane. They can run at speeds of up to 110 kilometres per hour over short distances. Cheetahs live in Africa and India and are perfectly adapted for a high-speed chase with their small heads, long legs and very slender bodies. But a cheetah's biggest head start is that it has claws that don't retract, which, together with its very hard paw pads, give it a running-shoe-like grip. Unlike other wild cats like lions and tigers, the cheetah does not lie in wait for its prey but chases it, tiring it out with twists and turns until its victim is too tired to run anymore.

THE BEST HIGH JUMPER

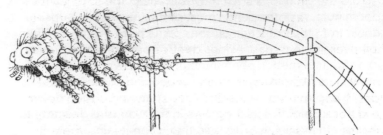

Fleas have very strong back legs that make them perfect for the long or the high jump. A flea can jump 100 times its own height. That's like you being able to jump to the top of a skyscraper in one mighty bound. Fleas use their jumping skills to leap on a new host to suck its blood.

In 2003, it was found that the jump of an insect called the froghopper could rival the flea's. Although the froghopper is only about 6 millimetres long, it can jump to heights of 70 centimetres!

THE FURTHEST TRAVELLER

Every year, a bird called the Arctic tern flies from the Arctic to the Antarctic and back again. Recently, to their surprise, scientists found they fly much further than previously thought. They attached a tiny tracker to the birds and found that they covered a distance of around 70,000 kilometres in a year. It seems impossible that these small birds, only around 20 centimetres long, can fly so far. Surprisingly, researchers have found that the birds spend a month or so at sea in the North Atlantic Ocean, possibly to feed before they resume their journey. On their return, they follow a winding route, but there is sense in this, as it seems they follow the prevailing winds.

The bar-tailed godwit, a wading bird with long legs, may not travel as far as a tern but it manages to travel from Alaska to New Zealand in just nine days without stopping – a distance of 11,000 kilometres.

THE OLDEST ANIMALS

Adwaita was an Aldabra giant tortoise from the Seychelles islands, who was brought to the Alipore Zoological Gardens in India in 1875, and died there in 2006. Carbon-dating on his shell after he died showed he was about 255 years old.

Even though Adwaita was clearly very old, he was not the oldest living animal ever. In 2007, a clam was dredged up off the seabed north of Iceland. This clam, given the name 'Ming', after the Chinese dynasty in power at the time it was born, was estimated to be a whopping 405 years old. This made the clam 149 years old when Adwaita was born. Unfortunately for Ming, it never got to celebrate its momentous birthday, as it had died by the time the scientists had worked out its age.

Clams are relatively easy to age compared to other animals, as they gain a ring on their shell each year. It is amazing to think that this clam was born when Elizabeth I was Queen of England.

THE BEST ESCAPE ARTIST

It may not have any bones in its body, but the octopus is a clever creature. It has a brilliant memory and, once it's learned how to do something, it doesn't forget. An octopus can work things out for itself, too.

Taken from a rock pool by a family in New Zealand, 'Octi the octopus' worked out how to open a bottle containing live crabs.

The boneless octopus is also a bit of a magician. If it finds itself in a tight spot facing a predator, it can scarper fast by squeezing through a hole no bigger than one of its eyes!

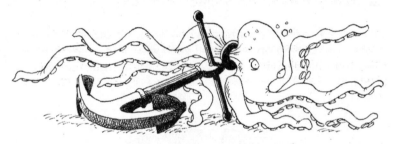

THE BEST DOCTORS

Maggots may look pretty ugly and be associated with stinking rotten food, but in fact they can be some of the best doctors around.

Even with the advances made in modern medicine, people can still suffer with infected wounds that will not heal. This is why some doctors in hospitals have brought back a very old and gruesome remedy, once used by the ancient Egyptians. They fill infected wounds with wriggling maggots and then put on bandages. When the bandages are removed, the maggots have eaten away the infected flesh and only a healthy clean wound remains, filled with much fatter maggots. The maggots are then removed and the wound is left to heal normally.

THE MOST MISUNDERSTOOD ANIMAL

Pigs are intelligent animals with an undeserved reputation for being dirty. It is true that they roll in mud, but this is to keep cool and clean. Pigs don't have sweat glands like humans do, so they can't sweat to help them cool down. A roll in the mud does the same job as sweating. The pigs cool off as the mud dries. Also, the mud helps get rid of any fleas or parasites on their skin, as these crack off with the dry mud.

Pigs aren't stupid either – they have long memories. Professor Curtis from Penn State University, USA, taught a group of pigs to jump over dumbbells, and sit next to and fetch different objects, such as frisbees. Three years later, the pigs still remembered what they had been taught.

Studies have shown that pigs can dream, recognise their names and even play video games with a joystick. They enjoy playing football, having a massage and listening to music. They also form close relationships, and prefer to sleep nose to nose.

EXTREME EATING HABITS

THE GROSSEST DINER

A housefly not only spits all over the food it lands on, it also makes itself sick on it, too. A housefly's mouth, known as a 'proboscis', is formed in the shape of a drinking straw, so it can only suck up liquid food. To make food mushy enough to eat, a fly spits saliva down the tube to start digesting it and then sucks it back up. If the food has not been broken down enough, the fly will sick it up and eat it all over again.

Another creature with gross eating habits is the vampire bat. They like the taste of warm blood from other animals and sometimes from humans. They wait until night time when their victim is asleep, then they look for an uncovered part of its body, like the soles of the feet. They make sharp incisions with their teeth and lap up the spilt blood like a cat laps up milk.

THE FINEST DINER

The flower-piercer birds of South America are particularly fine diners. Their preferred delicacy is the super-sweet nectar found very deep inside some flowers, making it hard to reach. The bird latches onto the flower with a little hook on the end of its upper beak and at the same time makes a small cut into the flower with its sharp lower beak. The bird then inserts its tiny tongue and, very delicately, sips the nectar.

THE WORST TABLE MANNERS

The Tasmanian devil is a carnivorous mammal found only on the island of Tasmania off the coast of Australia. It has a large head and powerful jaws that can crunch their way through almost anything. It crawls inside the carcasses of dead wallabies and wombats and eats them from the inside out. It eats everything – guts, fur, bones, the lot. It uses its front paws to cram lengths of intestine into its mouth – a bit like a very messy spaghetti eater! Someone once saw 22 Tasmanian devils feeding inside one dead cow. Its eating habits, however, are not why it is called a devil. It is called this because it terrifies people with its screeching cry.

THE SPORTIEST EATER

Some species of mongoose from Africa make eating reptile or bird eggs look like a fun game. The mongoose holds the egg in its front paws, opens its back legs, bends forward and hurls the egg through its legs, smashing it against a rock or a tree. Then it licks up the runny egg out of the broken shell.

THE GREEDIEST ANIMAL

The starfish has an appetite bigger than its small mouth can satisfy. When it discovers a tasty treat, like a snail or a sea slug on the sea floor, the starfish turns itself inside out by pushing its stomach out through its mouth, engulfing the prey. Its stomach then secretes juices that quickly digest the animal. When the food has been digested on the outside of its body, the starfish turns itself 'inside in' again.

THE BEST PARTY TRICK

The African egg-eating snake can swallow an egg whole. To eat the egg, which is too big for its mouth, it unhinges its lower jaw, pops in the egg and swallows. The egg slides slowly down the snake's throat, rubbing up against some sharp spikes, which slit it open. Then the snake swallows the yolk and coughs up the crushed shell.

THE STRANGEST CREATURES

THE LONGEST-LIVING HEADLESS CHICKEN

On the 10th of September, 1945, in Colorado, USA, Lloyd Olsen went into his garden to kill a chicken for supper. He didn't aim his axe very well and despite losing most of his head, 'Mike' the chicken didn't die. He just carried on as he had before, although Mr Olsen had to feed him through his neck with an eye dropper. This brainless bird grew from just over 1 kilogram to 3.5 kilograms and lived for another 18 months. He became so famous that people from all over the country paid to see him.

When Mike died, his body was examined and it was found that he had been left the small part of his brain that controlled his heart and his breathing and so was able to remain healthy. It is thought that without the rest of his brain he was unable to feel any pain or distress.

THE SMARTEST ANIMALS

THE CLEVEREST ANIMAL

Jane Goodall, the famous 'primatologist' (a scientist who studies apes), claims that chimpanzees are more intelligent than any other animal, apart from human beings of course, as they are able to use tools. They have been observed putting sticks in termite holes to catch termites and throwing objects as weapons.

There is a chimpanzee in Japan named 'Ai', or 'love' in Japanese, who has gone one step further. She is completely hooked on her computer. She loves computer games and has learned to solve complex problems involving streams of numbers.

A chimpanzee's brain works in a very similar way to a human's. Chimps share 98 per cent of our genes and even catch the same diseases we do. They are our closest living relatives.

THE BEST COMMUNICATORS

Dolphins love to talk. Just like people telephone or text their friends, dolphins use high-pitched sounds to communicate with other dolphins a long way off. Humans can only hear these sounds using special equipment.

Dolphins live in families called 'pods'. Female dolphins whistle to their babies continuously for three days after they are born to help them recognise the sound of their mothers.

Dolphins also use sound to navigate and to locate food – this is called 'echolocation'. They emit clicks using the 'melon', which is the rounded part of their foreheads. The sounds bounce off objects around them and the dolphins 'hear' the echoes through their lower jaws.

A MAN'S BEST FRIEND

Dogs can be the most devoted friends a person can have. This can certainly be said of 'Bobby', a Skye terrier, who belonged to a man called John Gray.

John was a nightwatchman in Edinburgh, Scotland. When he died in 1858, he was buried in Greyfriars churchyard and, for 14 years after his death, Bobby visited his master's grave every day, sometimes sitting at it for hours at a time. When Bobby himself died, he was buried as near to his master as was allowed – by the gate, just inside the churchyard. A statue and fountain were put up in Bobby's memory.

THE BEST MEMORY

Elephants have wonderful memories – which is useful as they can live for over 70 years. If an elephant is separated from a friend and they don't see each other for a number of years, when they do meet again they instantly recognise each other. There is evidence to suggest that they can even remember humans and bear grudges against people that have done them harm in the past.

Elephants also feel sadness. If a friend or a member of their family dies, they actually show grief. It is thought that elephants can remember trauma from their childhoods right into their adult life that can affect their behaviour and even turn them into hooligans.

THE BEST VOCABULARY

Koko the gorilla was born in 1971. From the age of one Koko, who lives in San Francisco Zoo in the USA, has been learning how to communicate with people. It is claimed that Koko can understand around 2,000 spoken words in English and can herself sign over 1,000 words using American Sign Language. Koko's IQ is thought to be between 70 and 95, which is pretty smart considering a normal IQ for a person is around 100. Koko loves playing with dolls and drawing.

THE BEST WEATHER FORECASTERS

Everyone knows that cats make excellent pets, but did you know that many people believe they may be the best four-legged weather forecasters?

It is thought that when cats lick themselves, it can mean fair, dry weather. In licking themselves, cats are in fact moistening their fur. When the weather is very dry, tiny electrical charges can build up in a cat's coat that can result in static electric shocks. By moistening their coats, cats may be trying to prevent this.

In the past, sailors would keep a cat on board ship, not only to keep control of rats, but also to forecast approaching storms. Some even believed that cats could control the weather and were capable of stirring up a storm with their tails.

THE MOST ENDANGERED SPECIES

THE LONELIEST TORTOISE

'Lonesome George' was, until his death in June 2012, the only remaining giant tortoise from the island of Pinta in the Galapagos Islands. George was taken into captivity in 1972 and, in order to preserve the species, the hunt was on to find him a suitable mate. Over the years, George had shown little interest in mating with tortoises from nearby islands. In July 2008, a female tortoise of a similar species, who had been George's companion since 1993, laid some eggs, but sadly they failed to hatch. It was hoped that the recent arrival of two new females would lead to the patter of tiny feet at long last, but George's death means his subspecies is now extinct.

THE BLACK RHINO

In 1960, there were 100,000 black rhinos in Africa. Today, there are less than 4,000. Rhinos are killed for the large horns on their foreheads which people grind up and use as medicine. In Asia, especially in China, people think the rhino horn reduces fever, although chemical tests performed show that the horn has absolutely no proven medicinal qualities.

THE BAIJI

Baijis, also known as Chinese river dolphins, live in the
Yangtze River system in China. They are thought to be the
most endangered member of the family of animals that
includes whales, dolphins and porpoises.

The last documented sighting of a baiji was in 2002, but when
experts searched for them again in 2006, none were found.
So this beautiful, intelligent mammal is now described as
'possibly extinct'.

THE GIANT PANDA

Giant pandas are among the rarest mammals in the world.
There are now only about 1,600 left living in the wild.

Pandas are sometimes killed for their lovely black and white
fur. However, the main reason pandas are dying out is
because forests of bamboo, their favourite food, are being
torn down to make way for roads and railways. The Chinese
government has set aside special reserves for the pandas,
where they can live and breed in safety.

THE TIGER

The tiger is the biggest of all the wild cats and possibly the most magnificent. People hunt it for its coat, its teeth and even its whiskers, which some people think will bring them good luck. But the worst threat to the tiger's survival is the loss of its habitat. There are thought to be less than 4,000 tigers left in the wild – mainly in China, India, Russia and Indonesia.

THE BELUGA STURGEON

This enormous fish can grow to be over 5 metres long and is considered to be one of the most valuable fish in the world. Sturgeons are killed not for their flesh, but for precious eggs that the females carry. Beluga eggs are called 'caviar'. Selling for as much as £58 for 10 grams, caviar is a delicacy and costs about ten times as much as 10 grams of silver!

THE BRAVEST ANIMALS

THE MEANEST MULE

Mules were known more for their stubbornness than their courage, until this incredible incident in Montana, USA. Two people were out riding when a cougar attacked their dog. The mule that one of the men had been riding, grabbed hold of the cougar and began whirling it round, banging its head on the ground. Then the mule held it to the ground by its throat and stamped on it. When it was satisfied the cougar was dead, the mule calmly walked back to its owner as if nothing had happened.

THE PLUCKIEST PIGEON

You know that many thousands of brave men fought in the Second World War, but have you heard about the parachuting pigeons?

In 1942, a British pigeon called Commando was dropped over France in a box attached to a small parachute. A spy working behind enemy lines found the box, placed important intelligence documents in the metal canister attached to Commando's leg, and set him free. The bird then flew with this vital information back across The Channel to England, dodging enemy fire as he went. He even had to evade hawks that had been specially trained by the enemy to stop these birdie bulletins reaching their destination.

Commando carried out 90 top-secret missions, and in 1945 was awarded a special medal for 'conspicuous bravery and devotion'. He was one of 200,000 birds used to carry messages during World War II.

THE MOST COURAGEOUS KANGAROO

The Richards family in Australia rescued a baby kangaroo, from her dead mother's pouch. They took her into their home and treated her as a pet, naming her Lulu.

One day, Mr Richards was working outside at their farm when he was knocked unconscious by a falling branch. When Lulu saw what had happened, she rushed back to the house and barked at the door until Mrs Richards came out. Then Lulu took her to where her husband lay unconscious. Later, Lulu was given a special award for bravery by the Royal Society for the Prevention of Cruelty to Animals. She is only the ninth animal to have been honoured with the award for her courage in helping Mr Richards.

THE MOST DANGEROUS ANIMALS ON LAND

MAN'S DEADLIEST ENEMY

The mosquito is the animal most deadly to man. Its bite transmits a variety of killer diseases, the worst of which is malaria. Every year up to one million people die from malaria. Most of malaria's victims are young children in Africa, where a child dies from the disease every 60 seconds.

THE DEADLIEST ARACHNIDS

Arachnids are a group of animals that includes scorpions and spiders, some of the deadliest and most feared creatures on Earth.

There are at least 1,400 types of scorpion, and all are venomous. Scorpions look a bit like lobsters, except that their curved tails are carried above their heads. The tail has a venom-releasing stinger at the end, which the scorpion uses to paralyse its prey. The most deadly of them is probably the death stalker scorpion, of North Africa and the Middle East. It hunts at night, eating insects, spiders and sometimes small lizards and snakes.

The most venomous spider in the world is the Brazilian wandering spider. This spider is also known as the banana spider because it has been found in shipments of bananas. Native to Central and South America, this spider can be fast and aggressive. The Brazilian wandering spider is particularly dangerous to human beings because, unlike a lot of other spiders, it does not have a web, so when it seeks shade from the sun it can find its way into people's clothes, or shoes. You have been warned!

THE MOST VENOMOUS SNAKE

The inland taipan is a snake that comes from Australia and produces the world's most lethal snake venom. Taipans can grow to a length of 3.7 metres. A bite from this snake contains enough venom to kill 100 people, or 250,000 mice.

When angry, the taipan flattens its head and waves it backwards and forwards. It can strike with such speed that its victims can be bitten several times before the snake retreats. Anyone bitten by a taipan has little chance of surviving without prompt medical aid, and many victims die within a couple of hours.

Although the taipan is the most venomous snake, it isn't the snake that kills most people, because it is actually quite timid and won't attack if you leave it alone.

THE SINGLE DEADLIEST CROCODILE

Crocodiles are thought to be responsible for more fatalities than any other predator that actually attacks people to eat them. The crocodile who could claim the title of the world's most deadly is a Nile crocodile named Gustave.

Gustave terrorised the people who live along the banks of the Rusizi River, in Burundi. Locals claim the crocodile has killed up to 300 people, though this is probably an exaggeration. The huge reptile is estimated to be more than 6 metres long and weighs over 900 kilograms. It has evaded many attempts to trap it and the last confirmed sighting was in 2008.

THE MOST LETHAL FROG

The golden poison frog might only grow to 4 centimetres long, but it contains enough poison to kill 10,000 mice or 10 to 20 humans.

Luckily, this poisonous frog tastes so awful that it has only one predator – a snake that has some resistance to its poison. The strange thing is, the frog does not produce its own poison. Scientists think the frog gets it from something it eats – probably a tiny beetle. If they are right, then this beetle must be one of the most poisonous creatures in the world.

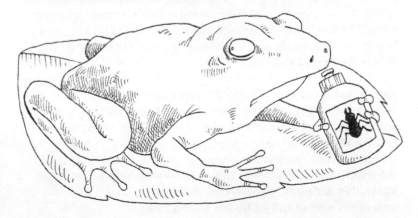

THE DEADLIEST MAMMALS

Hippopotamuses have a deadly reputation. They can be huge, weighing up to 3,628 kilograms and, though they live largely on plants, they can be very aggressive. They are territorial and will fiercely protect their young. Hippos can easily bite a man in two with their enormous jaws fearsome tusks.

Another mammal with a fearsome reputation is the lion. Lions are powerful animals, capable of breaking the necks of wildebeests with a single blow of one of their massive paws. An adult lion is strong enough to drag a carcass twice as heavy as itself. Lions will only attack humans when food is scarce, or when they are injured and cannot hunt faster prey. The deadliest lion struck in Tanzania in 2004. This one lion killed 35 people and it is thought he did this due to the discomfort of toothache.

Wild elephants have a far better reputation and are considered to be peaceful animals that look after each other and rarely attack humans. However, a male elephant can behave aggressively when looking for a mate, and female elephants will attack when their calf is threatened. Herds of elephants stampede when they feel threatened, or anxious. When this happens, people can be crushed under their enormous feet or gored by their long tusks.

THE DEADLIEST SEA CREATURES

THE DEADLIEST SHARK

The sea can be great fun to swim in but beware, there are some scary creatures lurking in the deep. The first deadly creature you might think of is the shark. The deadliest shark is the great white, the largest of all the marine predators. These massive hunters can grow up to 6 metres long and weigh over 2,000 kilograms.

Great whites are perfectly designed killing machines armed with rows and rows of teeth, lining up behind their front teeth. When a shark loses a main tooth it is replaced with one from the rows behind. The teeth have jagged edges and sharp points, so that they can easily saw through the flesh of their prey. Great whites are incredibly fast and can attack with such force that they can lift their prey clear out of the water.

Great whites are known to be aggressive and are attracted to swimmers. They mistake the movements of a swimmer with the thrashing of a wounded seal. However, great whites will usually only attack humans when there is a shortage of food or when defending its territory. Even though sharks have a man-killer reputation, according to the Florida Museum of Natural History, there have only been 263 attacks in the last 130 years or so, and only 69 of these were fatal.

THE MOST SAVAGE STINGRAY

Stingrays attack when they feel threatened. Unlike sharks, however, it is not a stingray's bite you need to fear. Although some stingrays can grow to a length of 4 metres, their mouths are very small. It is their tails that can be lethal. A stingray's tail has a 20-centimetre-long spear at its tip which is jagged like the blade of a bread knife and contains venom.

When the stingray is threatened, it will lash out with its tail spear. The wounds can be very painful, but are rarely fatal. People usually recover from an attack by a stingray within 48 hours. If, however, a person is struck on their chest or abdomen, they can die within minutes – from the wound rather than from the venom.

This is what happened to ecologist and TV personality, Steve 'the crocodile hunter' Irwin, in September 2006. The spear at the end of a stingray's tail pierced his heart as he swam above the fish in the sea off the coast of Australia. He died moments afterwards.

THE SCARIEST SEA SNAKE

Banded sea kraits have the strongest venom of all sea snakes. A banded sea krait can produce up to 15 milligrams of venom and only a fraction of that amount is a lethal dose for a human. The amount contained in just one bite is enough to kill more than three people.

Although they look like eels, sea kraits are real snakes – they have no gills and have to come to the surface of the water to breathe. They grow to a length of up to 1.2 metres.

The time to be most cautious of banded sea kraits is at night when they are most active and swim closest to the shore. They aren't aggressive, and their victims are usually fishermen who get bitten by accident when these deadly snakes get tangled in their nets.

THE DEADLIEST OCTOPUS

The blue-ringed octopus may only measure 20 centimetres across but just one bite can kill a man in minutes. When frightened, this octopus's pale rings suddenly turn bright blue. This is a warning for you to move away at once. The tiny octopus bites with its jaws and injects its saliva into the wound. The saliva contains one of the most dangerous toxins known to man. Luckily, blue-ringed octopuses are not aggressive and will only bite in self-defence.

THE MOST DANGEROUS JELLYFISH

If a normal jellyfish has ever stung you, you know how much it can hurt, but the pain would be nothing compared to the sting of a box jellyfish. Box jellyfish live in the Pacific Ocean, and each one contains so much venom that its sting can kill a person in just 3 minutes.

A box jellyfish can weigh up to 2 kilograms and has 15 tentacles that can trail up to 3 metres behind them. These tentacles are covered with 5,000 stinging cells, and contact with only a small number of these cells can kill.

THE BEST PARENTS

THE EMPEROR PENGUIN

Emperor penguins live in Antarctica. They don't migrate, but stay and breed during the worst weather conditions on Earth.

Around mid-May, each female emperor penguin lays one egg and passes it to its mate. The female goes off in search of food to feed the chick once it hatches. She will march for over 100 kilometres to reach the sea where she can find fish.

Meanwhile, the male keeps the egg balanced on his feet, under his feathers to keep it warm. He stays like this for 65 freezing days and nights, huddled with other dads against the terrible cold and wind. During this time the male doesn't eat a single meal. When the female returns, the male passes the egg back and almost immediately it begins to hatch.

It is said that emperor penguin parents can recognise the cry of their chick among a colony of thousands of chicks. Chicks that wander away from their parents are at risk from predators, but they may be 'adopted' by other adults.

THE BEST DADS

THE HIP-POCKET FROG

The hip-pocket frog, also known as the marsupial frog, comes from Australia. The female lays up to 20 white eggs, which she and the male look after together until they hatch.

The male watches the eggs for a few days until they hatch into tadpoles. When the tadpoles hatch, the male climbs amongst them and coats himself in the jelly from the hatched eggs. The tadpoles wriggle along their father's back until they reach two tiny slots in his skin. They wriggle through the slots into pouches. Here they stay for several weeks, feeding on yolk left over from the hatching, until they then pop out as fully-formed frogs.

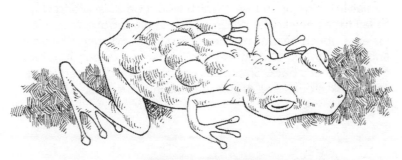

THE SEA HORSE

Sea horse fathers have a particularly close relationship with their unborn babies. They are probably the best example of fathers caring for their young in the animal world, because the fertilised eggs, from which baby sea horses emerge, develop inside the father's body, not the mother's.

The female deposits eggs into a special pouch beneath the male's tail, then developing embryos burrow into honeycomb-like structures inside the pouch, staying there until they are ready to be born.

THE BEST MUMS

THE NORTHERN ELEPHANT SEAL

Northern elephant seals are massive animals. An adult male can weigh up to 2,300 kilograms, and females up to 800 kilograms. The females give birth to single pups. They are devoted mothers and stay with their babies, going without food themselves, until the pups can survive without their mothers' milk.

They are such devoted mums, that if a female loses a pup, she will go to any length to get another one, even stealing a pup from another mother, or adopting an orphan.

THE KOALA

Koalas live high up in trees, which would be a very long way to fall for a baby koala. When a baby koala is born, it crawls inside a pouch near its mother's hind legs and stays there safe and sound for up to six months. When it comes out, it rides on its mother's back. She feeds her baby pre-digested leaves as this takes out some of the poisons in the leaves.

THE NILE CROCODILE

Nile crocodiles are fearsome predators but, surprisingly, make very loving mothers. They lay approximately 50 white eggs and bury them close to water, and guard them carefully for 90 days before they hatch.

When the eggs begin to hatch, the tiny, finger-sized babies begin calling for their mother. The female crocodile responds at once and gently helps to crack open any egg that isn't broken. She then picks each baby up one at a time in her fearsome jaws and carries it to a safe place near the water's edge. She continues to care for her brood in this nursery area for the next three to six months, bringing them food until they are old enough to feed themselves.

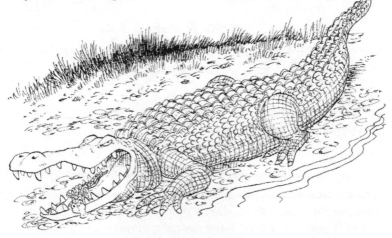

THE HUMPBACK WHALE

The female humpback whale is a big mum with a massive heart. She can grow up to 16 metres long and weighs 36 tonnes. Her heart alone can weigh 195 kilograms. But a humpback whale can be a loving and gentle mother. As soon as her calf is born she helps it to the surface with her flippers so it can take its first breath. She protects her baby from harm by nudging it with her fin to keep it close.

THE BEST ANIMAL TEAMWORK

A 'symbiotic' relationship is one in which two organisms of different species work together, each getting something from the other. Here are some of the best relationships.

THE BOXER CRAB AND THE ANEMONE

The boxer crab and the anemone have a very interesting relationship. The crab carries a pair of small anemones in its claws. These anemones have stinging tentacles and, when the crab sees an enemy, it waves the anemones around scaring it away. The crab returns the favour by dropping small scraps of food for the anemone when it is eating.

Some hermit crabs use anemones in a similar way. They can have anemones attached to their shells. This camouflages the crabs, making them look like rocks, while the anemones' stinging tentacles protect the crabs from predators.

THE PLOVER AND THE CROCODILE

It is hard to imagine a more dangerous job in the animal kingdom than being a crocodile's dentist. Crocodiles have long and powerful jaws filled with razor-sharp teeth that need to be kept clean. The Egyptian plover, a small bird with a pointed beak, is more than happy to help out. When a crocodile wants to have a bit of a clean and polish, all it has to do is come to the shore and open its enormous mouth. A plover will hop in and out, eating any annoying bugs and parasites lodged in the crocodile's teeth. When the bird is finished, it hops out of the croc's mouth and the crocodile goes on its way with a bright shiny smile.

THE OXPECKER AND THE RHINOCEROS

An example of a more complicated symbiotic relationship is that of oxpecker birds and rhinos. Oxpeckers are also known as tickbirds because they eat the ticks and other parasites that live on the backs of rhinos; the oxpeckers get food and the rhinos get rid of parasites. Unfortunately, Oxpeckers also pick existing scabs on rhinos' backs, reopening and enlarging the wounds. This makes the rhino vunerable to infection, which can be very harmful.

THE BEST AND WORST EYES

THE MANTIS SHRIMP

The only animal in the world known to be able to see all the colours in the spectrum is the mantis shrimp. Its sight is better than a human's, and its specialised eyes can see infrared and ultraviolet light. Scientists believe that this reef-dwelling crustacean can even see a type of light called 'polarised light' that no other animal is able to detect.

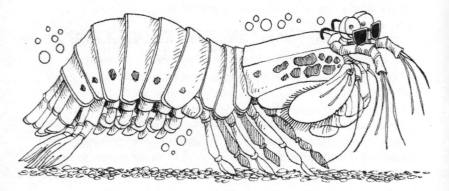

THE GHOST FISH

An animal that spends its whole life living in dark underground caves is called a 'troglobite'. The ghost fish, otherwise known as the Ozark cave fish, lives in springs deep in pitch black caves in the Ozark mountains in Arkansas, USA. It is almost unfair to accuse these fish of poor eyesight because they don't have any eyes – they don't need them. It is so dark in the caves where they live, that they wouldn't be able to see anything anyway. The Ozark cave fish has developed other means of hunting for prey and detecting danger. It has sensors on its body that can detect tiny movements and chemical changes in the water around them.

THE PEREGRINE FALCON

Experts believe that peregrine falcons have eyesight up to eight times more powerful than that of human beings. They can spot a seagull moving up to 8 kilometres away.

Peregrines are excellent hunters. They have very sharp 'binocular vision', which means that their two eyes work together to create a single image of an object. Not all birds have this type of vision, but without it, the peregrine falcon wouldn't be able to judge distances so accurately. They dive on their prey at speeds of up to 320 kilometres an hour, often killing the other bird instantly! At those speeds, super-accurate vision is vital.

THE HORNED TOAD

The horned toad isn't a toad at all. It is actually a lizard and is less commonly known as the short-horned lizard. This squat, spiny reptile uses its eyes to ward off predators such as wild dogs and coyotes. When threatened, the horned toad can squirt blood from its eyes to a distance of up to 3 metres. Not only does this frighten predators, the blood contains chemicals that make the lizard a particularly foul-smelling and unappealing snack.

THE COOLEST CAMOUFLAGE

THE GREATEST SUBMARINE DISGUISES

The stonefish is a master of disguise. It is perfectly camouflaged against a piece of coral, or a sand-covered rock, as it is mottled in green and brown spots. With very lumpy skin that can look like clinging bits of weed or algae, the stonefish is not only one of the most well-disguised fish in the world, it is also the most venomous. It has spines along its back that are able to inject venom that can cause paralysis and even death in its prey.

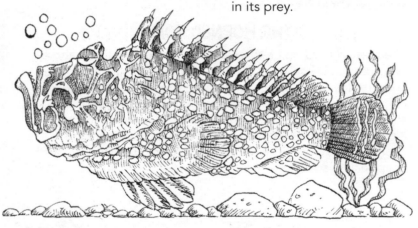

When it comes to changing colour, the octopus and the cuttlefish are the best. They can disappear in an instant, blending perfectly with their background. Alternatively, when they're in the mood, they can show themselves off with bursts of bright colour. Some even light up, with tentacles that glow in the dark.

An octopus's colour changes can also show what mood it is in – white shows fear, red shows anger, while brown means it is relaxed.

THE STICK INSECT

The stick insect has many tricks to avoid being seen. When it is motionless, it stretches its legs out in front of its head so that it looks like a leafless stick. When it moves, it uses a swaying motion, as if it were being blown in the wind like a twig. The stick insect's eggs look exactly like seeds so that predators don't notice them.

THE LEAF INSECT

Leaf insects have excellent camouflage. Their flat, green bodies look exactly like leaves, complete with the raised ribs and veins. Some even have an irregular shape, and look like a leaf out of which a caterpillar has taken a bite.

THE BIRD-DROPPING CRAB SPIDER

The bird-dropping crab spider pretends to be a bird dropping to protect itself from its enemies. It spins a small, lumpy disk made of silk. It attaches this to a leaf and then sits in the middle. The spider's body is covered with little bumps, which make it look like something a bird has left behind.

THE MOST EXTREME TRICKS OF NATURE

THE FROSTIEST FROG

The North American wood frog has an incredible skill to get itself through cold winters. As the nights draw in and temperatures drop close to freezing, the wood frog fills its veins with sugar and sits tight. The sugars in its blood act like a type of antifreeze that make it harder to freeze. If temperatures continue to fall, the frog is able to freeze – its internal organs protected by a surrounding layer of ice.

The frog's heart stops beating and it does not breathe. All of its organs literally stop dead. If you picked it up, it would feel like a frozen rock, but it is not dead. As spring approaches and the weather gets warmer, the frog begins to thaw, from the inside out. When it is completely thawed, its heart begins to beat again and it can get on with looking for a mate.

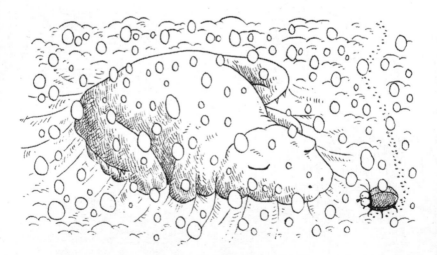

THE HOTTEST SURVIVORS

Over 2,000 metres down under the Pacific Ocean, just off the coast of Washington State, USA, lies a narrow vent that produces vast quantities of hot, sulphurous water. The water surrounding these vents gets to a scorching 80°C.

Unbelievably, scientists have discovered a species of worm living in these vents, at a temperature which would kill any other animal. It is known as 'the Pompeii worm', after the famous volcanic eruption in the town of Pompeii, Italy (see page 232). The worms look like little red palm trees and live inside a tube made of their own mucus. It is pitch black at these depths, and these worms live by eating bacteria that feed on the mineral-rich nutrients in the water around them.

THE DRIEST SURVIVORS

Brine shrimp live in salt pools and lakes where the water is so salty that they, and the algae they feed on, are the only things that can survive. When brine shrimp reproduce, they lay eggs called cysts. In times of drought, these eggs will dry out and lie on the lake beds for years. However, as soon as they are immersed in water, they instantly hatch out and are fully grown after eight days.

A fully grown brine shrimp is only 15 millimetres long, but its eggs are no bigger than the head of a pin.

THE FLASHIEST FISH

Flashlight fish live in dark caves in the Red Sea, where the bright lights from underneath their eyes can be seen up to 30 metres away. Flashlight fish do not make their own light. They have colonies of bacteria that are able to light up, living underneath their eyes. The fish use this light like the beam of a torch to find their prey and lure it towards them.

If the flashlight fish are in danger, they blink their eyelids to hide the light, and swim quickly away to safety. Flashlight fish can also use their light to confuse predators, flashing it up to 75 times per minute. When lots of fish start flashing at the same time, the keenest predator becomes confused.

THE FLASHIEST FIREFLIES

Fireflies are insects that twinkle in the night sky, but they're not flies at all – they're beetles. Fireflies have lights on the underside of their stomachs, which they use to signal to each other. The light is produced by special chemicals reacting in their cells. Fireflies control how bright their lights are by varying the amount of air that reaches their cells. In most species, both sexes flash messages to one another.

THE MOST PAINFUL ROMANTICS

There are two animals competing for the title of the world's most painful romantics – the praying mantis and the redback spider. Many believe the female praying mantis bites the head off the male when they mate, but this isn't always the case. Male mantids observed in captivity had nowhere to escape to after mating and, if the female was hungry, his number was up. In the wild many males do survive the process.

The female redback spider does eat the male while mating and the male actually helps her! He somersaults to place his body in front of the female's mouth as they mate. Scientists think that by eating the male the female gets extra nutrients that make her able to produce lots of eggs.

THE STRANGEST MAMMAL

The duck-billed platypus may have a strange-looking face, but that isn't the only thing that makes it unusual. The male duck-billed platypus is one of the only venom-producing mammals in the world. It has a poisonous spike on its ankles, which it can use to kill other animals, but it only does so in self-defence.

The females are very unusual, too. They are one of only two mammals in the world that lay eggs – the other is the echidna. After the eggs have hatched, the blind, hairless baby platypuses stay in a burrow, feeding on milk from tiny openings in their mothers' bellies. These odd-looking mammals are so unusual that when the first one arrived in Britain from Australia scientists initially thought it was a joke!

THE SMELLIEST MAMMAL

The striped skunk, found in the USA, has a chemical weapon sure to make any predator think twice about eating it. Whenever it feels threatened, or under attack, the striped skunk can spray anything it doesn't like with an oily, yellow liquid produced by two glands under its tail. It can spray up to a distance of 5 metres. The smell of the spray is foul and almost impossible to get rid of.

THE DOG WITH TWO NOSES

Dogs are already famous for their heightened sense of smell, which is many times better than that of human beings. Dogs are used to sniff out drugs and explosives and also to follow the scent of criminals to track them down. It has even been reported that dogs are able to sniff out cancer on people's breath.

The best of these sniffing sleuths may be a very rare breed of dog discovered in Bolivia, in 2005. The double-nosed Andean tiger hound has a split down the middle of its nose, so looks like it has two noses. Whether or not this gives it a better sense of smell is yet to be discovered.

FANTASTIC FOSSILS

THE BIGGEST FOSSILS

Some of the oldest and largest animals to have lived on this planet have been preserved as fossils. Dinosaurs first appeared on Earth around 215 million years ago. They came in all different shapes and sizes. Today, only fossils of their bodies still remain. The largest fossilised dinosaurs ever discovered are called sauropods. These giants were herbivores, which means that they only ate plants. Sauropods are thought to have been a little like modern giraffes, with very long necks used to reach the leaves on trees.

In December 2006, the remains of a type of sauropod called a turiasaurus were found in Spain. This turiasaurus is estimated to have been 30 to 37 metres long, and to have weighed between 40 and 48 tonnes. This makes it the largest dinosaur to have been discovered in Europe, but not the largest in the world. In the summer of 2006, fragments of another sauropod were discovered in Argentina. These remains are thought to be part of a titanosaur. Scientists estimate that the titanosaur must have been up to 40 metres long and to have weighed up to 100 tonnes.

THE BIGGEST MONSTERS ON LAND AND SEA

In 2007 a new dinosaur was discovered in North Africa. The 'carcharodontosaurus iguidensis' is thought to be even bigger than the famous tyrannosaurus rex. This dino-giant would have measured 14 metres long when fully grown, with teeth the size of bananas and shaped like steak knives for tearing its prey to smithereens.

Ferocious dinosaurs didn't just live on land. The pliosaurs were some of the largest marine predators that ever lived. It had large teeth, muscular jaws and huge paddles for pushing itself through the water. Richard Forrest, a leading dinosaur expert, claims that, 'A large pliosaur was big enough to pick up a small car in its jaws and bite it in half.'

One of the largest pliosaur skulls found was discovered in the cliffs at Weymouth, UK. It measures some 2.4 metres, which means the pliosaur was probably around 15 – 18 metres long.

THE MOST ANCIENT FOSSILS

A team of British and Australian scientists studying rocks found in Australia have discovered what may be signs of the earliest life on Earth in the form of what looks like single cell organisms in the rocks. The rocks are 3.4 billion years old, which would make these some of the oldest fossils ever found.

THE MOST ANCIENT TREES

THE EARLIEST TREE

Archeologists have found the first complete fossil of one of the world's oldest trees – a primitive plant, which, when growing 385 million years ago, looked like a palm tree, or tree fern. It is called a wattieza and grew over 140 million years before the dinosaurs. The tree fossil was found in a small sandstone quarry in New York where other interesting plant and insect fossils had already been found. It was discovered just in time, as the stone was about to be dug up to build roads. The wattieza was probably about 10 metres in height when fully grown. Its height helped it to survive because the palm-like trunk, topped with spreading foliage, was able to get the maximum amount of sunlight.

THE OLDEST FOREST

In 2010, repairs were made to the Gilboa Dam, New York State, United States, allowing researchers to re-examine the area, where tree fossils were found in the 1850s and 1920s. They were astounded by what they saw. Not only were root systems visible, there was also astonishing detail and the earliest examples of trees made of proper 'wood'. The Gilboa forest is 385 million years old.

Another example of an early forest is also found in North America. The Petrified Forest in Arizona is a forest of stone trees. It is over 220 million years old. Over millions of years, logs and the stumps were covered over by silt and sand carried by the rivers in the area. The wood rotted and was replaced by minerals, or dissolved rock, until all the wood had gone and only rock was left. The shape of the wood, even its growth rings, were preserved. This forest is sometimes called the Rainbow Forest, because the minerals that make up the petrified wood are brightly coloured and there are crystals of amethyst and yellow citrine clustering in cracks.

THE OLDEST LIVING TREE

Until recently the oldest living tree was thought to be the 5,000-year-old bristlecone pine in California. In 2004, however, Professor Leif Kullman of Umeå University, Sweden, reported a Norway spruce to be much older.

The spruce tree, measuring only 4 metres tall, has a root system that has been growing for over 9,550 years, though the part of the tree that grows above the ground is thought to be much younger. One reason the Norway spruce can reach such an old age is because even though the trunk can live for over 600 years, when it dies, the root system sends up a new one, so the oldest tree could live for a long time yet.

THE OLDEST GERMINATED SEED

A 2,000-year-old date-palm seed found in an ancient palace near the Dead Sea in the Middle East was germinated in 2005 and grew into a sapling. The ancient seed, nicknamed Methuselah after the oldest man in The Bible, was found in a jar into which the ancient inhabitants of the palace had thrown their date stones. It is hoped that this date seed may hold the key to ancient cures for which the date palm was famed.

THE BIGGEST AND BEST TREES

THE BIGGEST SEED

The biggest plant seeds can weigh around 20 kilograms and come from the giant fan palm of the Seychelles in the Indian Ocean. The tree is also known as the 'coco de mer' (coconut of the sea) because the trees often overhang the beaches and drop their giant seeds straight into the ocean. The seeds may then travel for thousands of miles before washing up on another shore. Despite their long journeys these seeds never grow into trees because the giant fan palm can only grow in the Seychelles.

THE TALLEST TREE

The tallest trees on Earth are the giant redwood trees in the Humboldt Redwood State Park, California, USA. They can take 400 years to mature and some of the trees in the park are thought to be more than 2,000 years old.

One of the tallest living tree is a giant redwood, named Hyperion, which is 115.2 metres tall. It is taller than the Statue of Liberty in New York, USA, or the height of 26 double-decker buses piled on top of one another. This leafy giant was confirmed as the tallest tree in 2006, when Professor Stephen Sillet climbed to the top and lowered down a measuring tape from the level of its highest leaf. The previous record holder was a tree named Stratosphere Giant which measured 113 metres tall.

THE FASTEST-GROWING TREE

The fastest-growing tree is the beautiful paulownia, sometimes known as the empress or princess tree. It flowers in April, and has masses of fragrant, foxglove-like flowers. The tree can grow as much as 3 metres in its first year, and reach a height of 15 to 20 metres in just three to five years. The wood is almost impossible to set alight and doesn't rot.

In Japan, there is an ancient custom to plant a paulownia when a baby girl is born. The tree is then cut down and made into a carved wooden cabinet when she is ready to marry.

THE MOST DANGEROUS TREE

The manchineel tree is found in Central America and the Caribbean. Touching its grey bark or leaves can cause painful blisters. If you sheltered under the tree in the rain, the rain would burn your skin after washing through the leaves. If you burnt its wood your eyes would seriously sting, and if you got the tree's sap in your eyes it could cause blindness. Needless to say, if you eat the fruit of this toxic tree, you could die.

THE SUICIDE TREE

There is a palm tree growing in Madagascar, which is a complete puzzle to scientists. The tree grows for up to 50 years and then one day it literally 'flowers itself to death'.

In 2006, a couple having a picnic noticed that a palm tree had suddenly sprouted a huge number of flowers and fruit. The flowers were dripping nectar and the tree was covered with birds and insects. It was a rare and wonderful sight. They went back to see the tree shortly afterwards, and were astonished to find it had collapsed and died. When scientists tested the tree's DNA, they discovered it was not just an unknown species, it was from an entirely new family of trees. So far only 100 other surviving 'suicide palms' have been found.

THE TREE-KILLING PLANT

The most ruthless tree-killing plant must be the strangler fig. It grows on the trunk of a 'host' tree, sending out a network of roots that completely enclose the host, stopping its sap flowing. The fig's leaves cover the host tree's leaves, taking all their sunlight. The host tree, now inside the fig plant, dies and rots, leaving the fig behind as a knobbly, hollow tube that can be over 50 metres tall.

Strangely, this big killer can't produce seeds without the help of a tiny wasp. The female gall wasp lays her eggs inside the fig's fruits. The fruits contain tiny holes just large enough for the wasp to squeeze into, but as she does, she loses her wings. Trapped inside, she lays her eggs and dies. The hole in the fruit closes up with the wasp inside. When the young wasps hatch, some chew their way out of the fruit. On the way they are brushed with pollen which they carry to other figs. This allows the strangler fig to breed and thrive.

THE BIGGEST RAINFOREST

The Amazon rainforest is the largest tropical rainforest on Earth. It stretches through eight countries in South America – Brazil, Colombia, Ecuador, Bolivia, Venezuela, Peru, Surinam, Guyana as well as the territory of French Guiana. The rainforest covers an area of approximately 6.6 million square kilometres – which is the equivalent of half the size of South America.

The rainforest is very hot and sticky and has an average of 2 metres of rainfall a year, whereas London's rainfall is just 60 centimetres a year. These warm, wet conditions make the Amazon rainforest a great place to live.

That is why it is home to more than half of all of the world's species of plants and animals. In just 6.5 square kilometres of the forest, you could find up to 750 different species of tree, 400 different species of bird and around 125 species of mammal, and an even larger number of different bugs and creepy crawlies.

Trees in the Amazon grow to around 30 to 35 metres tall and form a canopy high up above the forest floor. This provides shelter for some of the most unusual species on the planet.

The biggest rainforest on Earth also plays a massive part in regulating the world's climate. Gases released into the Earth's atmosphere surround it like a blanket. These are called 'greenhouse gases'. The right amount of greenhouse gases are important for regulating Earth's temperature. However, thanks to a growing population and more cars and factories, the amount of gases, such as carbon dioxide, being released is increasing, as if the blanket has got thicker. This means that Earth will be warmer as more heat will be trapped.

The Amazon rainforest absorbs more carbon dioxide from the atmosphere than anything else on the planet. The trees also produce more than 20 per cent of the world's oxygen. Without trees to do this, the world's climate could change forever. Humans are destroying this amazing forest at a shocking rate, chopping down trees to build houses, make furniture and create fields for cattle. As the trees disappear, the animals that live among them lose their natural habitat. In just one month an area about the size of New York was cleared in the Amazon rainforest. If the destruction continues at this rate, the rainforest will disappear in less than 70 years.

THE STRANGEST PLANTS

THE MOST BLOODTHIRSTY PLANT

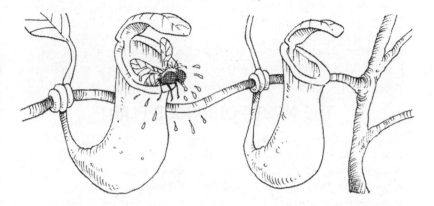

Most plants get all the nutrients they need from the Sun and from the soil around their roots. Some plants, however, have developed more gruesome ways of finding a meal. The pitcher plant is a cunning carnivore, or meat-eater, that has developed a bloodthirsty way of adding to its diet and making up for the poor soil conditions it lives in.

The pitcher plant's favourite food is flies, and it has leaves that are perfectly designed to catch them. They form slippery tubes which are half filled with a lethal nectar. The fly is attracted to the plant because of its bright colour and sweet nectar held within. It buzzes into the plant and, before it knows what is happening, has slithered down the tube into the pool below. Unable to escape up the slippery walls, the fly drowns. The plant then releases digestive juices into the pool, which dissolve the fly so that it can be absorbed. Sometimes, larger animals such as frogs and mice try to drink from the plant and meet the same watery end.

THE VENUS FLYTRAP

The Venus flytrap plant spells death for insects. It has leaves made up of two nearly circular parts with spiny teeth along their edges. The two parts are hinged together to form a trap. On the surface of the leaves are short stiff hairs. When an insect touches these hairs, the leaves snap shut in a split second. The plant produces sap that digests all the soft parts of the insect. After about ten days the plant opens its leaves, allowing the remains of the insect to be blown away by wind or washed away by rain. If an object is trapped by the leaves that isn't food, like a tiny twig or bit of gravel, the plant will wait about 12 hours and then open its leaves and 'spit' it out.

THE MOST POISONOUS PLANT

The castor bean is one of the deadliest of all plants. An adult who eats one, or maybe two, castor beans could die within three or four days.

Castor beans contain a poison called ricin. Ricin stops the cells in the human body from reproducing. It only takes a drop the size of a pinhead to kill an adult.

In 1978, a Bulgarian writer, Georgi Markov, died in London after a single pellet of ricin was injected into his leg (see page 57). It is believed that Markov's assassin used an adapted umbrella to inject the pellet while he waited for a bus. Markov died three days later.

THE SMELLIEST FRUIT

The durian fruit looks like a live hedgehog and smells worse than a dead one. The smell of a durian has been compared to rotting fish, unwashed socks, and the inside of a dustbin on a hot day. Its smell is so putrid that in Borneo in Asia, where the durian grows, people have been banned from carrying them on public transport or taking them into hotels. However, in many parts of the world the durian is considered a delicacy and, if you can get it past your nose, it tastes delicious.

THE SMELLIEST FLOWER

You wouldn't want to receive a bouquet of titan arums, also known as the 'corpse plant', because they smell of dead bodies and rotting fish. As well being the smelliest flower in the world, the titan arum is also the largest and can grow to over 1.3 metres across. It has a central spike that is up to 3 metres tall.

The plant itself can live for about 40 years, but it produces only one flower, two or three times in its lifetime. This giant bloom lasts for about 36 hours before collapsing.

THE SMELLIEST SELF-HEATING SURVIVOR

The skunk cabbage is a stinky plant with amazing tricks up its sleeve. Unlike other plants that prefer to flower in the spring and summer, the skunk cabbage flowers in winter to avoid competing with other plants. Instead of attracting bees and butterflies, the skunk cabbage is equipped with a foul fragrance to attract the type of flies usually drawn to rotting animals. These flies aren't in such short supply in winter when there are no bees and butterflies around.

Skunk cabbages grow in wet, boggy areas where temperatures can fall well below freezing. However, unlike other plants, they don't die when they are covered in snow and ice. Instead, these amazing plants heat up by converting starch into sugars in their roots. This chemical reaction produces heat, so inside the skunk cabbage's cone of flowers, it can be a cosy 22°C, even though it is below freezing outside. Enough heat comes from it to melt the surrounding snow. Even flies don't like the cold, so a nice warm place that gives off its favourite smell is too good to miss. Just as long as the fly brings pollen with it, the plant is happy.

THE MOST EXPENSIVE DISEASED PLANT

Today some flowers can be expensive to buy, but in early 17th-century Holland, some flowers could cost more than a man could earn in a whole year. The country went crazy over tulips, with rich people competing with each other to own the rarest and most beautiful plants. The price of tulip bulbs went up and up, until the precious bulbs were changing hands for huge sums of money. Bulbs could even be exchanged for whole areas of land, complete with buildings, cattle, sheep and pigs.

The most expensive tulip was the semper augustus. A single bulb was sold for 6,000 florins, which is as much as it would take a man 40 years to earn. This red-and-white striped tulip was so highly prized that it had its portrait painted. Scientists later found out that the tulip's stripes were the result of infection by a virus.

THE MOST FANTASTIC FUNGI

Many people think that fungi are plants, but they aren't – they form a kingdom all of their own. You can find fungi everywhere and they come in all shapes and sizes, from microscopic moulds to edible mushrooms to what is thought to be the biggest living thing on the planet.

THE BIGGEST LIVING THING

A giant fungus called a 'honey mushroom' has been found growing underground just 1 metre below the Malheur National Forest in Oregon, USA. This humongous fungus is estimated to cover 8.9 square kilometres, about the size of 1,665 football pitches, and is one of the largest living thing in the world found so far.

You can see small bits of the fungus showing above the ground. Experts aren't quite sure how old it is, but they know it is very old and started growing at least 2,400 years ago. Amazingly, this giant will have started off in the same way as a mushroom you might have in your dinner, from a single seed-like 'spore', so small it isn't visible to the naked eye. The scientists first noticed it when the trees in the forest began to die. The honey mushroom thrives by sucking water and nutrients from the tree's roots and the trees are unable to survive.

THE MOST EXPENSIVE FUNGUS

The white truffle is considered to have one of the most delicious flavours in the world, but it is very rare and difficult to find. This makes it the world's most expensive fungus and perhaps the world's most expensive ingredient. It grows underground next to the roots of oak and hazel trees and is found mainly in Italy. In 2010, a pair of rare white truffles weighing 900 grams and 400 grams sold for an incredible £210,000, making them worth £150 per gram!

Truffles are difficult to find. They have a strong smell, but as they are buried under the ground, people can't sniff them out. Pigs were once used to look for them, but they could eat as many as you found and your fingers could be in danger trying to pry a juicy specimen out of a pig's mouth. Now, trained dogs are used instead. If you don't have a dog, another clue is a suillia fly that lays its eggs around truffles. Suillia flies hover over the spot where the truffles are growing, looking for a place to lay their eggs.

THE MOST FATAL FUNGAL FAMILY

Mushrooms can be tasty treats. They come in lots of different shapes and sizes and can be delicious additions to any meal, but beware: there are some really nasty ones out there, too.

There are around 70 species of poisonous mushrooms or toadstools, some of which can look just like edible mushrooms, but are as deadly as any poison known to man. The deadliest toadstools of them all come from the same group or genus, called *Amanita*. The death cap mushroom is as scary as its name. The death cap grows to around 15 centimetres tall and its cap is between 5 and 10 centimetres across. The death cap comes in a variety of colours from brown or dark green to pale yellow, so can be hard to identify. It has a sweet smell, like roses, but just one bite of a death cap can kill. Between 6 and 24 hours after eating a death cap the victim experiences excruciating stomach pain, sickness, and becomes very thirsty as their body tries to use as much water as it can to flush out the poison. In half of the cases the victim will fall into a coma and die. There is no known antidote for the death cap mushroom, though some treatments have been successful.

Also in the *Amanita* genus are the group of mushrooms called the 'destroying angels'. These pure white, innocent-looking mushrooms may seem very delicate and pretty, but, like their close relative, they can cause a painful death. As little as half a cap can kill an adult.

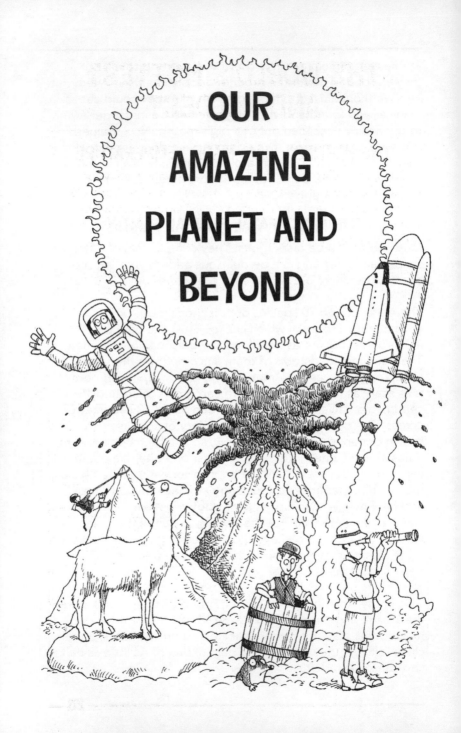

OUR
AMAZING
PLANET AND
BEYOND

THE WORLD'S HOTTEST AND COLDEST

THE HIGHEST MAN-MADE TEMPERATURE

In 2010, scientists working with the Relativistic Heavy Ion Collider, a huge 'atom-smashing' machine in New York, USA, produced plasmas (superheated gases) whose temperature exceeded 4 trillion °C. This is incredible when you consider the Sun's interior is only about 15 million °C.

This is hot enough to make the particles within the nucleus of an atom break down, and is thought to resemble the state of the Universe soon after the Big Bang. The scientists created the plasmas by smashing atoms of gold together at almost the speed of light.

THE HOTTEST NATURAL TEMPERATURE

The hottest natural temperature ever recorded on Earth was in El Azizia, Libya, on the 13th of September 1922. The temperature reached 58°C. Scorching desert winds called the Ghibli can raise temperatures in this part of the world by 40°C to 50°C in the space of a few hours.

The Sahara Desert in North Africa is big – very big. It covers a third of the whole continent, measuring 8.6 million square kilometres – it is almost the same size as the USA. It is the largest hot desert in the world. The highest temperature ever recorded there was 58°C. In a single day, the temperature can range from below freezing to 50°C. These extremes of hot and cold, combined with the dry, dusty winds, make the Sahara a place where few plants and animals can survive.

The Sahara is very hot, but it isn't the heat that makes it qualify as a desert. It is the lack of rain. The average rainfall in the Sahara is less than 50 millimetres. London's rainfall, for comparison, is 600 millimetres a year.

THE LARGEST DESERT

The title of the world's largest desert does not go to the famous Sahara – there are two larger deserts on Earth. Antarctica measures 14 million square kilometres of actual land plus an extra 18 million square kilometres if you include the sea of ice that engulfs it in winter. The title 'desert' is awarded to areas because of low rainfall, and the Antarctic has an average rainfall similar to that of the Sahara. Some areas of the Antarctic haven't seen rain for millions of years. The Arctic icecap is also larger than the Sahara, measuring around 15 million square kilometres in winter.

THE COLDEST NATURAL TEMPERATURE

The coldest temperature ever recorded on Earth was – 89.2°C at a science laboratory called Vostok Station in Antarctica, on the 21st of July, 1983. The temperature there reaches its lowest during the winter months of July and August, when it is dark even during the day.

THE WORLD'S DEEPEST

THE DEEPEST PLACE

Challenger Deep is the deepest point on Earth, lying almost 11,000 metres below the surface of the Pacific Ocean. Challenger Deep forms part of the Mariana Trench, off the Marianas Islands, and was pinpointed as being the deepest point on Earth in 1951.

On 26th March 2012, the film director James Cameron undertook a two-hour descent into the Mariana Trench in his submarine called *Deepsea Challenger*. There, he explored the ocean floor for four hours, crouched inside his cramped craft. After his speedy ascent back to the surface he said, "It was absolutely the most remote, isolated place on the planet."

To give you an idea of how deep the Mariana Trench is, if you put Mount Everest (see page 220) into the trench there would still be 1,600 metres of water over the top of it.

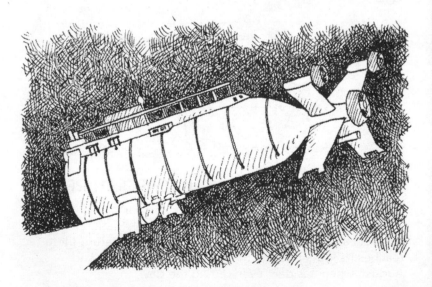

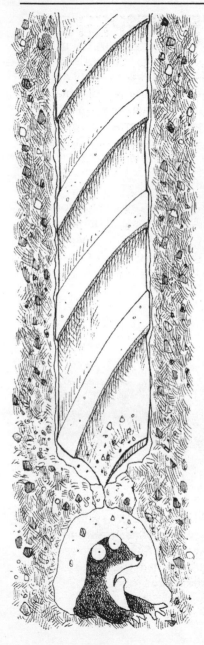

THE DEEPEST MAN-MADE HOLE

Drilling began on the Kola Superdeep Borehole, on Russia's Kola Peninsula, in May 1970. Scientists hoped to learn more about what made up the Earth's crust. The drills chewed away for 23 years, until they reached rock that was too hot for the drill-bits to function properly. Drilling finally stopped 12.26 kilometres below ground level.

THE DEEPEST BURIAL CHAMBER

The Valley of the Kings in Egypt is the burial site of the kings and queens of Ancient Egypt. The deepest of the burial chambers is that of the pharaoh Seti I.

Seti I's tomb was discovered in 1817, by Giovanni Belzoni. The tomb was found at the bottom of a 136-metre-deep shaft. A false burial chamber had been built above it to confuse tomb robbers. Sadly, it didn't prevent the actual tomb from being robbed and vandalised. Some experts think that parts of Seti I's tomb still remain undiscovered.

THE DEEPEST CAVES

Every spring for 20 years, determined cavers have been pushing themselves to descend deeper and deeper into the Cheve cave, in Mexico's Sierra de Juárez region. They are sure that this cave is the deepest cave in the world – they just haven't proved it yet. Exploring the massive cave is a bit like climbing Mount Everest in reverse. Base camps are set up for overnight stays, as it already takes cavers three days to get back up to the surface, and they haven't even reached the bottom yet.

Until they reach the bottom of the Cheve cave, the record for the deepest cave stands at 2,191 metres and belongs to the Krubera Cave in the Republic of Georgia. However, as the cave's entrance is on a mountain, when cavers reach the bottom, they are only 12 metres below sea level.

The world's longest cave is the Mammoth Cave system in central Kentucky, USA. The total length of its limestone passages is not known, but so far about 627 kilometres have been explored. Some cave experts believe the cave system will eventually prove to be 900 kilometres long.

THE LOWEST PLACE ON THE EARTH'S SURFACE

The lowest place on the Earth's surface is located on the shore of the Dead Sea. It lies at just over 400 metres below sea level, and it is getting even lower. Scientists have calculated that the level of water in the Dead Sea is falling by up to a metre every year, taking the altitude of the shoreline even lower.

The Dead Sea gets its name because it is so salty that almost nothing can live in it. Instead of sand round the edges, there are thick layers of white salt crystals. You can't really swim in the Dead Sea either – the salt makes the water so dense, you just float.

THE WORLD'S HIGHEST

THE HIGHEST MOUNTAIN

Almost every book of facts you read will list Mount Everest as the world's highest mountain. However, this information is not as straightforward as it might seem.

The title of the world's highest mountain can be awarded in different ways. It could be given to the mountain which has the biggest distance between its bottom and its top. Alternatively, the mountain whose peak is furthest away from the centre of the planet could claim the prize. However, the mountain to receive either of these titles is not Everest.

Mount Everest comes in at 8,848 metres, and certainly wins the title of the mountain whose peak is the highest point above sea level. However, the tallest mountain from base to peak is Mauna Kea, Hawaii, USA. From its underwater base to its peak it measures 10,203 metres, which makes it over 1,000 metres taller than Everest.

The shape of the Earth is known as an 'oblate spheroid', which means it is squashed like a ball that has been sat on. The Earth bulges around the equator – the imaginary line that runs around the middle of the planet. The land at the equator is approximately 21,000 metres further from the centre of the Earth than the land at the North or South Poles. Mount Chimborazo, Ecuador, is located very close to the equator. Its peak is only 6,310 metres above sea level, which makes it a full 2,540 metres shorter than Mount Everest. However, if you measure the distance between its peak and the centre of the Earth, that distance is over 2,000 metres greater than the distance between the centre of the Earth and the peak of Everest. Does this make Mount Chimborazo the highest mountain in the world?

THE HIGHEST MOUNTAINS ABOVE SEA LEVEL	
Everest, Nepal	8,850 metres
K2 (Chogori), Pakistan	8,607 metres
Kanchenjunga, Nepal	8,598 metres
Lhotse, Nepal	8,511 metres
Makalu 1, Nepal	8,481 metres

THE HIGHEST SEA STACK

A sea stack is a steep section of rock, separated from the mainland by sea. These stacks rise vertically from the water like pillars.

Ball's Pyramid rises from the sea off Lord Howe Island, 700 kilometres northeast of Sydney, Australia. At 548.64 metres, it is the highest sea stack in the world. It was formed, along with the rest of the island, when a massive underwater volcano erupted about 7 million years ago.

THE WORLD'S LONGEST

THE CITY WITH THE LONGEST DAYS AND NIGHTS

The city of Tromsø, Norway, is 350 kilometres inside the Arctic Circle. It is on the island of Tromsøya, connected to the Norwegian mainland by a wide tunnel and a bridge. Tromsø has the longest 'day' of any city because in the summer, from the 21st of May to the 21st of July, the Sun does not set, but stays above the horizon. This is called the 'Midnight Sun', because the Sun can still be seen shining at midnight.

Tromsø also has the longest 'night' of any city because in midwinter, from the 21st of November to the 21st of January, the Sun does not rise above the horizon. During these few months there is no daylight at all, apart from a very brief bluish twilight in the middle of the day.

Even though Tromsø is so far north, the climate is not that cold. Warm air currents called the 'gulf stream' flow around the island preventing the temperature from getting too low. The average temperature in winter is −4°C, and in summer it is 12°C. The record for the highest summer temperature in Tromsø is 30°C – as warm as Greece or Spain.

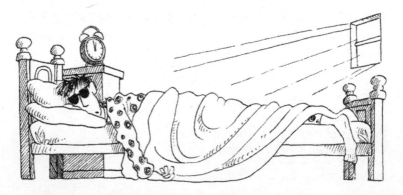

THE LONGEST NATURAL BRIDGES

Natural bridges and arches are very challenging to measure and compare as they are not uniform in shape. Until the formation of the Natural Arch and Bridge Society (NABS), measurements of natural bridges were not very accurate. NABS came up with a formula to measure the bridges so that their sizes can be compared. Fairy Bridge, located in a remote corner of China, has been declared by NABS as having the longest span at 90 metres.

Also topping its list is Landscape Arch, in Utah, which has a span of 88 metres.

Utah has around 2,000 natural arches, carved by the elements from the sandstone rocks. One of the most impressive is Rainbow Bridge. This incredible sandstone arch crosses over Bridge Canyon, 19 kilometres northwest of the Navajo Mountains, in southern Utah, USA. The distance from the top of the bridge to the bottom of the canyon is 94.18 metres, and the arch of the bridge measures 84.7 metres long. The Navajo Indians revere Rainbow Bridge as a sacred monument.

THE LONGEST COASTLINE

Canada has the longest coastline of any country in the world at 202,080 kilometres – this includes the coast of the mainland and the sum of the coastlines of 52,455 Canadian islands. There are oceans on three sides of Canada: the Pacific in the west; the Atlantic in the east; and the Arctic Ocean bordering the northern coastline. In the south, Canada is bordered by the USA.

Canada is the second largest country in the world. However, for its size it has quite a small population, at just over 32 million people. In comparison, Britain, a small country, has a population of over 60 million.

THE LONGEST RANGE OF MOUNTAINS

The Andes mountain range runs along the west coast of South America, stretching from north to south. At 7,245 kilometres long, it is the longest range of mountains in the world and one of the highest. The Andes are divided into three regions – north, south and central. The climate is different in all three.

The northern region of the Andes is located near to the equator and is hot and wet, with large stretches of rainforest. The southern region is colder as it is nearer to the Antarctic.

THE LONGEST RANGE OF MOUNTAINS UNDER THE SEA

The global mid-ocean ridge system is the longest chain of underwater mountains. They wrap around the world like the seams on a ball, for a distance of more than 65,000 kilometres. The largest is the Mid-Atlantic Ridge. It stretches for 16,000 kilometres from the Arctic ocean all the way down to the southern tip of Africa.

In the 1950s, oceanographers mapped the range using the latest sonar equipment of the time. They also found deep ocean canyons, trenches, volcanic mounds and coral reefs. The sea bed isn't just flat, boring stretches of sand – it has many of the features we have on land, and some are on a much grander scale. Much of it is yet to be explored.

RECORD-BREAKING RIVERS

THE LONGEST RIVER

The Nile and its tributaries, which are the smaller rivers that feed into it, is the world's longest river, stretching an incredible 6,695 kilometres from Burundi to the Nile Delta in the Mediterranean. It is generally thought of as Egypt's river, and it does flow through Egypt, but it also passes through eight other countries.

Even a river as mighty as the River Nile has to start as a trickle somewhere. The lure of adventure drew many famous explorers in the 19th century into a race to discover where that trickle started, known as the 'source of the Nile'. In 1862, John Speke found that the river flowed out of Lake Victoria, shared by Kenya, Tanzania and Uganda, but the true source, further upstream feeding into Lake Victoria, remained unknown until quite recently. Water travelling from this newly discovered trickle – a mountain stream in Burundi near the equator – takes three months to reach the Mediterranean Sea.

THE MIGHTIEST RIVER

At 6,695 kilometres, the Nile is the world's longest river, but not by much. The River Amazon in South America is 6,400 kilometres, only 295 kilometres shorter than the Nile. It could be described as a mightier river than the Nile because the Amazon transports over 100 times more fresh water to the sea than the Nile does. In fact, the water that comes out of the Amazon's mouth makes up one fifth of all the water carried by all the rivers around the world.

The Amazon's source is high up in the Andes mountains in Peru. It travels through Venezuela, Ecuador and Bolivia on the way to its estuary in Brazil. The delta, at the mouth of the river where it meets the sea, is 200 kilometres wide. Some researchers believe that the Amazon may have another source that would make the river even longer than the Nile.

The water flows out of the mouth of the Amazon at a rate of 180,000 cubic metres of water per second. The volume and sheer force of all the water flowing out of the Amazon is so great that freshwater samples can be taken 150 kilometres out to sea. To appreciate the vast volume, you should compare this to the outflow of the Nile, which is only 1,600 cubic metres per second – 112 times less!

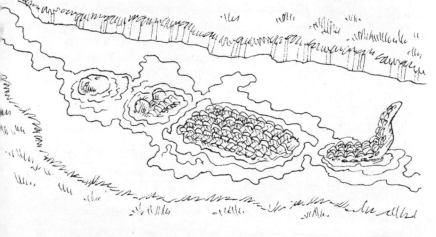

THE MOST AMAZING WATERFALLS

A waterfall is formed when one part of the ground, across which a river is flowing, suddenly drops away and the water falls almost straight down.

MOST RECENTLY DISCOVERED FALLS

Yumbilla waterfall in Peru was only discovered by scientists in 2007, though of course the people who have lived beside the falls for centuries always knew it was there. The waterfall has four massive cascades, which, when combined, measure 895.4 metres tall.

Peru's previous record-holder, the Gocta waterfall, just up the road from Yumbilla, was itself only discovered in 2002. Doesn't this make you wonder if Peru might have a few even taller waterfalls hidden away?

VICTORIA FALLS

The Victoria Falls in Zimbabwe earns the title of the biggest waterfall in the world. It is 1,708 metres across and it drops between 90 and 107 metres into the Zambezi Gorge. An average of 9.2 million litres of water cascades over the edge of the falls every second at peak season. Because Victoria Falls is so wide, the water drops in a vast curtain. The thunder of the spray when it hits the gorge below is incredibly loud. Local people call the falls 'Mosi-oa-Tunya', which means 'the smoke that thunders,' and for many people the place has magical qualities.

The first European to see the falls was the explorer David Livingstone in 1855. An island in the river is named Livingstone Island in his honour.

NIAGARA FALLS

Niagara Falls is the second biggest waterfall in the world and millions of people visit the site every year. It consists of three waterfalls – the American Falls, the Bridal Veil Falls and the Canadian Horseshoe Falls. An incredible 2,832 cubic metres of water tumble over the falls every single second during peak-time hours. In winter, if the temperature stays below freezing for long enough, ice and slush flowing over the falls cause an incredible ice 'bridge' to form across the river below the falls.

In the past, acrobats entertained tourists by walking on tightropes across the falls – one even crossed a wire carrying another man on his back. In 1901, a 63-year-old teacher named Annie Taylor was the first person to go over the falls in a barrel.

ANGEL FALLS

Angel Falls in Venezuela cascades over a flat-topped mountain from a height of 979 metres, making it the world's tallest waterfall. The falls are 500 metres across at the base.

The waterfall was unknown outside Venezuela until the American aviator, James Crawford Angel, flew over them in a small plane in 1933. On a return trip, he tried to land his plane there, but crashed. He and his companions took 11 days to trek down the mountain to safety.

THE MOST VIOLENT VOLCANOES

THE LARGEST ACTIVE VOLCANO

Mauna Loa is the largest active volcano on the planet. The name means 'long mountain', and it stretches for 120 kilometres, covering half of the Big Island of Hawaii. The base of the volcano is on the sea bed and, from there to the summit, the volcano rises around 17 kilometres.

Mauna Loa is also one of the most active volcanoes on Earth. It has erupted 15 times since 1900. During an eruption in 1984, lava flowed down the mountain, stopping only 6.5 kilometres from the town of Hilo. At the moment, the volcano is fairly quiet, with watchers only detecting a few rumblings.

MOUNT VESUVIUS

Mount Vesuvius, Italy, is possibly the most dangerous volcano in the world because it is located so close to the city of Naples, home to over three million people. Although Vesuvius hasn't erupted since 1944, it is still considered active and could erupt again in the future.

The most famous eruption was in AD 79, when white-hot ash covered an area of 4 square kilometres, completely burying the Roman cities of Pompeii and Herculaneum. The eruption was thought to have lasted 19 hours and buried Pompeii under 3 metres of ash. Almost all of the city's inhabitants perished, but as the ash settled, it smothered everything, preserving it for hundreds of years.

Today, if you visit Pompeii, you can see the remains of the town – the homes people lived in and the paintings on their walls. You can even see the casts of people lying frozen in time in the positions in which they fell when fumes and ash overcame them.

MOUNT ST HELENS

On the 18th of May 1980, Mount St Helens in Washington State, USA, became world famous. The volcano erupted with such force that it took everyone by surprise, even the scientists who had predicted the eruption. The explosion was as powerful as that of 27,000 atomic bombs and lasted 9 hours. The eruption was triggered by an earthquake – the force of the blast blew the top off the mountain and caused a huge landslide.

400 million tonnes of hot ash and dust were ejected into the sky. It blocked out the sunlight and choked rivers, causing floods and mudflows. Though 57 people lost their lives, many people living nearby had been warned the volcano was going to erupt and, luckily, had left their homes.

BEFORE   **AFTER**

KRAKATOA

Indonesia is a country that has more than 130 active volcanoes. When the volcano Krakatoa erupted in August 1883, it made the loudest noise ever recorded and was heard 3,110 kilometres away in Perth, Australia.

A series of huge waves called 'tsunamis' caused by the explosion washed away 165 coastal villages on Java and Sumatra, and at least 36,417 people died and thousands more were injured. Two thirds of the island of Krakatau was destroyed. Since 1927, eruptions have produced enough volcanic material to form a new island. Still small, just 2 kilometres across, it has been named Anak Krakatau – which means 'Child of Krakatoa'.

THE WORST NATURAL DISASTERS

FOREST FIRES

Forest fires can start for a number of reasons – by a lightning strike, campfires getting out of control, or they can even be started deliberately. Some forest fires start by themselves – this is known as 'spontaneous combustion'. One of the places they happen most is in Australia where they are called 'bushfires'.

In 1983, over 100 fires raged across 4,000 square kilometres of land, destroying property, wildlife, crops and killing 75 people. In 2009, 173 people died in what became known as the 'Black Saturday' bushfires. Australia has many eucalyptus trees and the oil in their leaves burns easily, so the fire spreads from tree to tree. Animals died if they couldn't run away fast enough. Kangaroos and emus move pretty quickly, so most escaped, and wombats survived by burrowing underground. Unfortunately, the slow-moving koalas were worse off and perished in large numbers.

The eucalyptus trees fare far better than the animals in bush fires. They need fire for their seeds to germinate. Their leaves and bark burn, but the trees re-grow quickly.

TROPICAL CYCLONES

Tropical cyclones can cause widespread destruction and death. They are huge storms that start over warm tropical seas. Their best-known features are violent winds and heavy rainfall, which can lead to storm surges, when water is forced towards the shore by the strong winds. During a severe cyclone gusts of wind may exceed a speed of 320 kilometres per hour.

A truly catastrophic tropical cyclone hit Bangladesh, which was known as East Pakistan at the time, on the 13th of November 1970. Winds of up to 230 kilometres an hour caused a massive storm surge. The storm surge travelled many miles inland, sweeping away villages and ruining crops. Many of the buildings in the villages were wooden shacks and stood no chance in the flooding – the water level in some areas rose as much as 12 metres. It is estimated that more than 300,000 people died in the disaster.

Cyclones are given human names, such as Betty, Andrew or Florence, for example.

A list of names is chosen, the first one starting with the letter 'A' and then continuing through the alphabet. One list will use girls' names, the next boys' names. If a storm has been named 'Betty' for example, the next will be given a boy's name, beginning with a 'C'.

EARTHQUAKES

When the Earth suddenly shakes it is called an earthquake. The shaking is caused by forces known as 'seismic waves' moving through rocks in the Earth's crust. The surface of the Earth isn't made of one single piece of rock, but of a number of massive pieces, known as 'tectonic plates' of rock, like a jigsaw. When these vast pieces of rock move against one another a huge amount of pressure builds up. This pressure is usually released when the plates of rock split and move – producing seismic waves and causing an earthquake.

The size of an earthquake is measured on a scale called the Richter scale, which assigns it a number according to its strength. The earthquake with the largest magnitude since records began struck Valdivia, Chile, in 1960. Some sources say it measured 9.5 on the Richter scale – fewer than three earthquakes a year measure over 8 on the scale. Approximately 130,000 homes and buildings were destroyed, making over two million people homeless. Some estimates put the death toll as high as 6,000 people.

An undersea earthquake on the 26th of December 2004, off the west coast of Sumatra, Indonesia, triggered a series of tsunamis, which killed more than 230,000 people.

TSUNAMIS

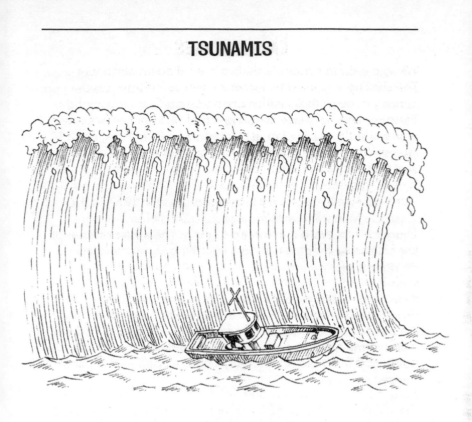

A tsunami is a massive wave, often caused by an earthquake in the sea floor. One of the worst tsunamis hit the coast of Indonesia in 2004. According to a geological survey, the earthquake that caused it had a force equal to that of 23,000 atomic bombs.

The earthquake created massive waves that swept towards land. These waves measured up to 15 metres high and travelled with such speed that within hours they had reached the coastlines of 11 different countries.

On 11th March 2011, a tsunami killed 16,000 people in Japan. Radiation escaping from the damaged Fukushima nuclear reactor has caused ongoing problems in the region.

AVALANCHES

An avalanche is when a large amount of material such as snow and ice slides down the side of a mountain, getting faster and faster as it goes. Like many natural disasters, an avalanche happens with very little warning. Some avalanches of snow may exceed speeds of up to 130 kilometres an hour, and 150 people are killed every year by avalanches in North America and Europe.

The worst avalanche in US history occurred in 1910, in the Cascade Mountains in Washington, USA. Two trains were caught in a blizzard and forced to stop. The avalanche swept the trains and their passengers into the gorge below, killing 96 people.

One of the worst recorded avalanches was in 218 BC, when Hannibal was crossing the Italian Alps with his elephants on his way to conquer Rome. A massive avalanche engulfed the army. Some historians say it caused the deaths of 18,000 soldiers, 2,000 horses and many of the elephants. Hannibal himself survived.

THE WORLD'S OLDEST FEATURES

THE OLDEST ROCKS

Most scientists agree that the Earth is about 4.6 billion years old. When it was first formed it was a boiling ball of molten rock and toxic gas, constantly bombarded by rocks attracted by the new planet's gravity.

As the Earth cooled and water evaporated into the planet's atmosphere, the liquid rock of the Earth's surface hardened to form a crust. This new crust was made up of a number of plates, just as it is today. The plates float on liquid rock, called the Earth's 'mantle', and are constantly shifting, pushing against each other to wear away old rock and pulling away from each other forming new rock. Volcanoes errupt and reshape the Earth's surface. This means that scientists think that all of the first rock that made up the Earth's first crust has since been worn away and recycled.

Some of the oldest rocks ever found were discovered in Australia by Simon Wilde and his team. They found tiny grains of rock estimated to be around 4.4 billion years old. These pieces are thought to be some of the first rocks ever formed.

THE OLDEST LAKE

Lake Baikal in Siberia is record-breaking in many ways. Formed 25 million years ago and 1,637 metres deep, it is the oldest and deepest lake in the world, containing one fifth of the world's fresh water. It contains 22 islands and is surrounded by mountains. Of the 330 rivers that flow into the lake, only one, called the Angara, flows out of it.

Lake Baikal is home to over 1,500 species of plants and animals that are found nowhere else in the world.

THE OLDEST ACTIVE VOLCANO

Mount Etna, on the island of Sicily, Italy, is estimated to be around 350,000 years old, making it the world's oldest active volcano. Most volcanoes are less than 100,000 years old. There is a record of Etna erupting as far back as 1500 BC, and it has been active ever since, last erupting in 2012.

In 2000, 'volcanologists', people who study volcanoes, observed several white rings of steam, up to 200 metres across, drifting out of the top of the mountain. It is thought they were caused by rapid pulses of gas being forced out through a narrow vent in the side of the volcano.

THE WORLD'S NEWEST FEATURES

THE NEWEST SALTWATER LAKE

On the 20th of November 1980, Lake Peigneur, in Louisiana, USA, was a very ordinary shallow lake, with an oil rig in the middle. The next day, none of the above was true.

On the 21st of November, oil workers made a rapid retreat when their oil rig began to sink. Once they had made it across the lake to safety, the workers looked back to see the huge platform of the rig and a vast lifting device called a derrick sink without trace into a lake that was only 3.5 metres deep. The water began to swirl, faster and faster, forming a whirlpool half a kilometre across. Another oil rig was swallowed up, as was 70 acres of land, some trees, a few large lorries and a car park.

A 19-kilometre-long canal joined the lake to the Gulf of Mexico. The whirlpool began to suck water out of the canal into the lake – with it went eleven barges that had been tied up on the canal. The whirlpool then began to suck seawater from the Gulf of Mexico along the canal. In just two days, the 3.5-metre-deep freshwater lake turned into a saltwater lake that was up to 400 metres deep in places.

How did this happen? Workers on the oil rig had accidentally drilled into the tunnel of a salt mine that was 500 metres below ground. The lake water flooded into the tunnels and made more room for itself by dissolving the salt tunnel walls and supporting pillars, bringing down the roof and washing it all away. The whirlpool that this collapse had created swallowed 13 billion litres of fresh water in just 3 hours.

Amazingly, despite the incredible danger and the amount of destruction, no-one above or below ground received so much as a scratch ... apart from the oil company, who had to pay tens of millions of dollars in compensation. Ouch!

THE NEWEST ISLAND

Land may seem very permanent, but the truth is that coasts are eroding into the sea and new land is being created all the time. New islands can be formed by volcanoes spewing out molten rock and lava, or bubbling mud that eventually emerges above the surface of the ocean.

Since 2011, a volcano has been spewing lava and gases into the air off the coast of El Hierro, one of the Canary Islands. This could form a new island, or extend the southern part of El Hierro. Scientists are keeping a keen eye on developments.

There is often some doubt with new islands that are formed by volcanic action whether they are permanent or just massive lumps of floating pumice – if there is still volcanic activity it is very dangerous to study them closely!

THE MOST FREQUENTLY NEW ISLAND

Ferdinandea, a volcanic island off the coast of Sicily in the Mediterranean, has held the title of the newest island in the world more than once, because now and again it just disappears.

Ferdinandea is only visible when the volcano is actually erupting – otherwise it lies just below the level of the sea. It has appeared and disappeared many times in its history. In 1831, the island appeared and was quickly claimed by four different countries! It conveniently disappeared again before anyone could decide who owned it.

In 1987, Ferdinandea lay just below the surface of the ocean and was bombed by a US pilot who mistook it for a Libyan submarine.

THE WEIRDEST WEATHER

THE STRANGEST THINGS TO FALL FROM THE SKY

You wouldn't bat an eyelid if rain or snow fell from the sky, but here are some more unusual things to have rained down:

- Jellyfish in Bath, England, in 1894.
- Ducks, woodpeckers and canaries in Louisiana, USA, in November 1896.
- Worms in Louisiana, USA, in July 2007.
- Tiny frogs in Odzaci, Serbia, in June 2005.

THE MOST AMAZING FLYING BABY

Tornadoes are columns of air that spin very fast. They move across the ground and cause some of the strongest winds on Earth. They have been known to suck things up, from large amounts of water from the ocean to whole houses. On the 4th of September 1981, a tornado struck Ancona, a port in Italy, where a baby was asleep in its pram. The tornado sucked the pram 15 metres into the air and carried it for 90 metres, before setting the pram safely back on its wheels. It is said that the baby, far from being upset, hadn't even woken up!

THE FREAKIEST HAILSTORM

Hailstones are lumps of ice and are formed when droplets of water in the air are repeatedly carried upwards by updrafts and downwards by downdrafts. If the ice is carried upwards and downwards a number of times, layers of ice are added and hailstones can get bigger and bigger.

Hailstones are usually smaller than 2.5 centimetres, but the biggest recorded to date weighed 1 kilogram. It fell in the town of Vivian, South Dakota, in 2010 and it measured 20.5 centimetres across. In July 2002, in Henan Province, China, hailstones as big as hens' eggs killed 22 people and injured 200 others.

THE MOST COLOURFUL SHOWERS

On the 25th of July 2001, it rained over the district of Kerala, India – the rain was bright red. The red rain didn't just fall once, but many times until September. The rain was so bright that it even stained people's clothes.

Most experts think that the red rain was due to dust and sand in the atmosphere, but Dr Godfrey Louis, a scientist in Kerala, claims that the red rain is evidence of life on other planets. He believes that the red particles had come from a passing meteorite or comet and were tiny alien bacteria!

THE STRONGEST WIND

In 1996, on Barrow Island, Australia, during tropical cyclone Olivia, winds of 408 kilometres an hour were recorded.

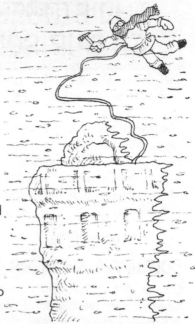

Before that, the strongest wind was recorded on the summit of Mount Washington, USA. During a 1934 storm there, gusts reached 372 kilometres an hour. The staff who recorded the wind speed did so in very tricky conditions. They were using an instrument called an 'anemometer', but first a brave team member had to climb onto the roof of the observatory, to clear the anemometer of ice!

THE DEADLIEST SNOWSTORMS

In 1972, about 4,000 people died in Iran after up to 8 metres of snow fell in parts of the country.

During a blizzard in Nebraska, USA, in 1888, 500 people froze to death. A fast-moving storm from the Arctic caused temperatures to drop to $-30°C$, in a matter of hours. The Nebraska blizzard is sometimes referred to as the 'Schoolhouse Blizzard', because during the snowstorm many children were trapped in their schools.

In February 2010, snowstorms paralyzed much of the USA. Snowfall records were broken, with more than 30 centimetres falling overnight in Washington on the 5th February. It was America's worst snowstorm for more than 90 years. President Obama dubbed it 'snowmageddon'.

THE BIGGEST AND BEST IN OUR SOLAR SYSTEM

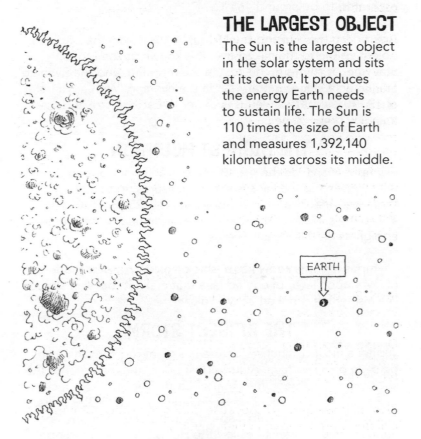

THE LARGEST OBJECT

The Sun is the largest object in the solar system and sits at its centre. It produces the energy Earth needs to sustain life. The Sun is 110 times the size of Earth and measures 1,392,140 kilometres across its middle.

EARTH

THE LARGEST PLANET

Jupiter is the biggest planet in our solar system, more than twice the size of all the other planets combined – it is over 11 times larger than Earth and measures 142,984 kilometres across its middle.

THE HOTTEST PLANET

Venus is the hottest planet in the solar system, but it isn't the planet closest to the Sun – Mercury is closer. Venus is hottest because the Sun's heat passes through its atmosphere but then can't escape. The heat builds up, and the temperature is estimated to be around 465°C.

Apart from the Sun and the Moon, Venus is also the brightest object visible to the naked eye. It is known as the Morning Star when it shines in the east in the morning, and the Evening Star when it shines in the west in the evening. With a diameter of 12,100 kilometres, Venus is closer to Earth in size and mass than any other planet.

THE HIGHEST MOUNTAIN

Olympus Mons, on the planet Mars, is an enormous volcano, the biggest in our solar system. It measures up to 624 kilometres across and rises approximately 25 kilometres above the surface of the planet, making it nearly three times as high as Earth's Mount Everest.

Olympus Mons is known as a 'shield volcano' as it is made up of layer upon layer of cooled lava that make it round in shape like a shield. It is not an active volcano.

THE BIGGEST STORM

Jupiter's most distinctive feature is a giant red spot that can be seen on its surface. At its widest point, the diameter of the spot measures three times that of Earth. The spot is in fact a giant gas hurricane that has been raging for up to 350 years. The winds reach incredible speeds, up to 360 kilometres per hour. In 1990, a satellite called the Hubble Space Telescope was launched into orbit around Earth. Since then Hubble has sent pictures back to Earth of two more red dots on the surface of Jupiter.

THE FIRST IN SPACE

THE FIRST ANIMALS

The very first animals in space were fruit flies. They were sent into space on board an American rocket launched in 1947. The purpose of the mission was to investigate the effects of radiation exposure and to assess how human astronauts might be affected.

THE FIRST SATELLITE

In the 1950s, the USA and Russia, which was then called the Soviet Union, raced against each other to be the first country to get an artificial satellite into space. Russia won with the launch of a satellite called *Sputnik* on the 4th of October 1957. It was only the size of a large beachball and weighed 83.6 kilograms, but its importance was immense, marking the start of the 'space age'.

WHOOSH!

THE FIRST CHIMPANZEE

The first chimpanzee in space was named Ham. He flew in the *US Mercury Space Craft* in 1961 which was launched from Cape Canaveral, in Florida, USA. Happily, Ham survived his trip.

THE FIRST PEOPLE IN SPACE

Russian Major Yury Gagarin became the first human being in space on the 12th of April 1961 on a spacecraft called *Vostok 1*. He was also the first person to return from space, landing near Engels, Kazakhstan. Two farm workers looked up to see a parachutist descending with no sign of an aircraft above. When they asked the parachutist if he had come from outer space, Major Gagarin replied, 'As a matter of fact, I have!'

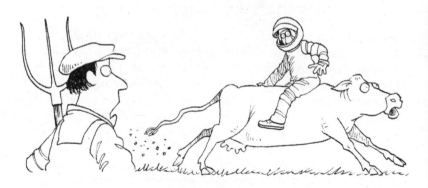

On the 16th of June 1963, Valentina Tereshkova became the first woman to go into space aboard the Russian spacecraft *Vostok 6*. The mission was top-secret, because the Russians did not want to be beaten to this 'first'. Even Valentina's mother did not know where her daughter was going until she heard on the radio that she was already there. Valentina still holds the record for the youngest woman in space – she was only 26 years old, and was chosen because of her love of parachuting.

THE FIRST DOG IN SPACE

The first dog in space was Laika, a Russian dog on board *Sputnik 2*, in November 1957. Laika had been found living as a stray on the streets of Moscow. Sadly she died, when *Sputnik 2* malfunctioned.

THE FIRST SPACE STATION

The first space station, *Salyut 1*, was launched by the Russians on the 19th of April 1971. Its purpose was to study the effect of being in space for a long time on the human body. It was equipped with a laboratory, scientific equipment, and an area for relaxation and exercise. The first spacecraft taking cosmonauts to work on *Salyut 1* was launched six weeks later, and the cosmonauts spent 23 days on board.

THE BIGGEST SPACE STATION

The International Space Station (I.S.S.) is the largest space station orbiting Earth. Work began on it in 1998. It has taken 13 years to complete at a cost of $100 billion. The 450-tonne station has room for seven crew members and a vast array of scientific equipment. It orbits 350 kilometres above our planet and can be seen from Earth with the naked eye, which means without a telescope. It travels at a speed of 27,700 kilometres per hour and orbits the planet 16 times a day. In May 2012, the first commercial rocket, *Falcon 9*, travelled to the space station, carrying supplies in a capsule named Dragon.

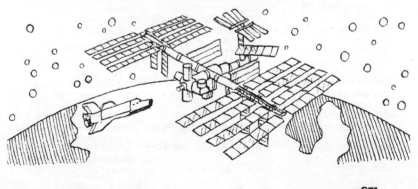

INDEX

ACKNOWLEDGMENTS

The author and publisher would like to thank the following organisations, the main sources for verification of information in The World's Best Book. All have proved to be excellent, brimming with reliable facts, and all are great ports of call. Most of these organisations maintain websites, where you can find further information:

The Aldo Leopold Foundation
Arizona State University
BBC
Beijing Olympic Games 2008
British Film Institute
Bronx Zoo
Central Intelligence Agency (CIA)
Channel 4
CNN
The Corrie Ten Boom Museum
The Daily Telegraph
The Darwin Awards series by Wendy Northcutt (Orion)
Der Spiegel
Encyclopædia Britannica
European Space Agency
Florida Museum of Natural History
Forbes
GoldMoney
The Guardian
The Independent
The International Olympic Committee
Internet Movie Database
Israel Times
MI5
Museum of Hoaxes
National Aeronautics and Space Administration (NASA)
National Center for Biotechnology Information
National Geographic
National Oceanic and Atmospheric Administration
National Security Agency (NSA)
Natural Arch and Bridge Society
Nature
New Scientist
New7Wonders
Niagara Parks
Nobel Foundation
The Nova Scotia Museum
Penguin Books
Population Reference Bureau
The Royal Society for the Protection of Birds (RSPB)
Smithsonian National Zoological Park
Songwriters Hall of Fame
The Spectator
The Telegraph
TIME Magazine
The Times
UK Office for National Statistics
UNESCO World Heritage Centre
US Census Bureau
US Department of State
US Geological Survey (USGS)
US Green Building Council (USGBC)
Webster's Dictionary
The World Health Organisation
World Wide Fund for Nature (WWF)